# Reconstructing American Law

# Reconstructing American Law

Bruce A. Ackerman

Harvard University Press
Cambridge, Massachusetts, and London, England   1984

This book is printed on acid-free paper, and its binding materials have
been chosen for strength and durability.

*Library of Congress Cataloging in Publication Data*

Ackerman, Bruce A.
    Reconstructing American law.

    Includes index.
        1.  Law—United States—History and criticism.
2.  Lawyers—United States—History.    3.  Law and politics
—History.    4.  United States—Politics and government—
1933–1953.    I.  Title.
KF380.A23    1984
ISBN 0-674-75015-2 (alk. paper)        349.73        83-12864
ISBN 0-674-75016-0 (pbk. alk. paper) 347.3

*For Arthur Leff*
*who understood that form was substance*

---

# Acknowledgments

THIS BOOK GROWS out of a decade-long conversation with my friend Mirjan Damaska, who will be developing some common themes in a forthcoming book on comparative law. I am also indebted to my colleagues at Columbia, Yale, and elsewhere for their thoughtful comments on one or another draft—most especially Vince Blasi, Robert Burt, Guido Calabresi, Harold Edgar, Don Elliott, Don Gjerdingen, Kent Greenawalt, Mark Kelman, Henry Monaghan, George Priest, Peter Schuck, Benno Schmidt, Peter Strauss, and Richard Stewart. A shorter essay, containing parts of Chapters 1, 3, 4, and 5, will appear in the *Yale Law Journal*, whose editors provided many helpful suggestions.

Kate Gorove helped with the footnotes, and Yvonne Tenney handled countless secretarial burdens with sensitivity and intelligence. As always, it is my wife, Susan, who has contributed most to this project through her deep understanding and unconditional support.

A grant from the Bernard H. Kayden Research Fund at Columbia University aided in the final revision of the manuscript.

# Contents

# · 1 ·

# Law in an Activist State

BY SAYING that we live in an activist state, I mean to mark a special feature of our self-consciousness: an awareness that the very structure of our society depends upon a continuing flow of self-conscious decisions made by politically accountable state officials. So conceived, the sources of our activist consciousness are several. Most obvious is the general recognition that our society's continued existence depends upon the military sanity of its political leadership. Second, and only slightly less pervasive, is the belief that the nation's economic welfare depends upon steering decisions made in Washington, D.C.—both at the macroeconomic level and through the regulation of particular sectors of economic life.[1] Finally, there is the widespread

1. This recognition must be distinguished from the particular ways a political administration discharges its steering responsibilities. Thus,

acknowledgment that the distribution of wealth and status is a central issue for political debate and determination. Poverty, racism, and sexism are not inexorable givens; they are the consequences of systematic practices in which state officials are self-consciously involved—from the moment at which they grant or deny an impoverished mother a free abortion to the moment at which Medicare sustains, or fails to sustain, the last effort to prolong life.

It is within this context of social perception—a context that gained its historical reality during the administration of Franklin Roosevelt—that I mean to situate the evolving legal culture. In looking back upon the New Deal, I will not attempt an appraisal of the substantive merits of any of its particular initiatives. Instead, I shall consider whether, after fifty years of arguing out the particular meanings of bits and pieces of activist law, lawyers can begin to see larger patterns in the professional effort to make sense of our existing legal situation. This exercise will suggest that the transformation of legal discourse engendered by the New Deal is deeper than one might initially suppose. Not only has the rise of the activist state forced lawyers to argue about new fact-patterns; it is also leading them to revise the very pattern of a professionally competent "statement of the facts." Not only has the profession been obliged to recognize the legitimacy of new values; lawyers are also beginning to conceive the nature of value controversy in a new way.

---

the Reagan administration does not deny the need for a coherent economic policy, but asserts, rather more stridently than some of its recent predecessors, that *its* comprehensive program will at last lead us to the promised land. Similarly, it has proved singularly incapable of generating political support for a massive return of regulatory authority to the States. See Mashaw & Rose-Ackerman, *Federalism and Regulation*, in THE REAGAN ADMINISTRATION'S REGULATORY RELIEF EFFORT: A MIDTERM ASSESSMENT (URBAN INST. forthcoming, 1984).

Although cultural diffusion is a complex and uneven affair, the new forms of factual description and normative evaluation are slowly becoming familiar to larger and larger groups within the profession. Talk of market failure and externality, Pareto efficiency and Rawlsian maximin, are no longer dismissed as hopelessly idiosyncratic. When arguments invoking these and other such notions are introduced into legal conversation, some of the participants have heard similar talk before; others are vaguely aware that such rhetorical maneuvers have been used elsewhere to win arguments in one or another administrative agency or legislature or court. Although most of the bits and pieces of the new rhetoric originated in universities, I shall not be treating them as if they were an odd set of trendy topics in law and economics and philosophy and other esoteric sciences. Instead, what we are witnessing is the birth of a distinctive form of legal discourse—a professionally stabilized rhetoric that increasing numbers of lawyers will be obliged to master if they hope to translate their clients' grievances into a language that powerholders will find persuasive; a new language of power, premised on a distinctive set of attitudes toward fact and value, that I shall call Legal Constructivism.

Not that I expect this birth announcement to excite general jubilation. The propagation of a new language of power cannot fail to be a traumatic event for a profession whose stock and trade is persuasive argument. Most obviously, the new form of law-talk threatens countless lawyers with the risk of professional incompetence if they fail to rise to the Constructive occasion in their practice before agencies, legislatures, and courts. More insidiously, the new discourse poses a threat to the profession as a whole: Does not the very effort to talk law in a new key suggest some deep disappointment with the old way of doing justice? These clear and present dangers to lawyerly self-esteem will provoke endless efforts at professional reassurance. The new law-talk will be continually exposed as a sham and repeatedly condemned as immoral. Particularly crude and insensitive applications of the new learning will be greeted with poorly concealed delight by lawyers who wish to dismiss the movement as aberrational and thereby avoid the need for the analytic retooling it seems to demand.

The transparent obscurantism of many of the critics, however, should not obscure their challenge to my claim that there *is* something in all this smoke of legal disputation to be fired up about. And so it will be my first task to induce you to suspend the disbelief naturally provoked by my thesis and to explain why our legal generation has been challenged by history to engage in a rare act of collective creation: to construct a new language of power that does justice to the aspirations for justice of our fellow citizens.

This will require us to begin by looking backward to the efforts of an earlier generation of lawyers to make sense of the New Deal and its aftermath. For it is only in this way that we may confront the historically rooted prejudices that must be transcended before Constructive lawyering can seem a central professional enterprise. Chapter 2, then, presents a reinterpretation of the jurisprudential movement that reached its climax with the New Deal: Legal Realism. During the 1930s, the Realists presented themselves, and were generally perceived,[2] as the pro-

2. For an important debate that helped prepare the way for the received interpretation of Realism's significance, see Pound, *The Call for a Realist Jurisprudence*, 44 HARV. L. REV. 697 (1931); Llewellyn, *Some Realism About Realism—Responding to Dean Pound*, 44 HARV. L. REV. 1222 (1931). The relationship between Pound and the Realists is thoughtfully explored by White, *From Sociological Jurisprudence to Re-*

fession's enfants terribles—debunking cherished legal myths with devastating effect. This undeniable aspect of Realism, however, should not blind us to the paradoxical character of its ultimate contribution to legal discourse. With a half-century's hindsight, Realism has come to seem profoundly conservative, not radically iconoclastic. Rather than transforming traditional legal discourse, the Realist critique allowed the profession to survive the New Deal without reconstructing its basic conceptual equipment. Rather than encouraging lawyers to confront the distinctive challenges posed by the rise of an activist state, Realism permitted the profession to evade them in good conscience.

It is precisely these evasions that Chapter 3 means to emphasize by moving from historical reflection to a more conceptual form of analysis. I aim here to explore, in general terms, the way in which the legitimation of an activist state fundamentally reshapes the lawyer's conversational agenda, forcing the profession to address new questions in a new way within a changing institutional setting. Only then will we be in a position to understand how the rising forms of Constructivism both destabilize the Realistic accommodation to the New Deal and allow a deeper understanding of the activist legal world in which we find ourselves. Chapter 4 describes the way in which the new legal discourse redefines the very notion of a competent "statement of the facts." Chapter 5 describes the perplexities generated by the new form of argument over legal value. The essay closes with glimpses into the future of legal argument.

*alism: Jurisprudence and Social Change in Early Twentieth Century America,* 58 VA. L. REV. 999 (1972); and taken up again at note 15 of chap. 2. See also W. RUMBLE, AMERICAN LEGAL REALISM 9–47 (1968).

# · 2 ·

# The Realist
# Legacy

A HALF-CENTURY AGO, our legal system was reeling under
one of the greatest shocks in its history. Although
America had experienced many depressions before, it had
never confided political power to a leadership so evidently
willing to respond by questioning the legitimacy of laissez
faire itself. While the ideological challenge was plain
enough in statutes like the National Industrial Recovery
Act,[1] the more insidious threat to the legal culture came
from an unending series of statutes that claimed more
modest goals—ranging from soft money to regulated securities, from collective bargaining to government pensions, from AAA to WPA. These New Deal creations did
not, of course, represent the first time an American gov-

1. For a sensitive discussion, see HAWLEY, THE NEW DEAL AND THE
PROBLEM OF MONOPOLY 19–148 (1966).

ernment had sought to manage the money supply or provide for worker security or regulate monopolies. While many New Deal programs did represent great leaps forward, I am not interested in debating the precise extent to which particular interventions were prefigured by Populist or Progressive achievements.[2] Even if it were possible to hunt out some sort of precedent for most New Deal initiatives, this would not undercut the unprecedented character of the New Deal challenge to legal discourse.

For that challenge resided precisely in the sheer quantity, not just the quality, of New Deal legislation. Before the New Deal, it remained professionally plausible for the thoughtful lawyer to view self-conscious state intervention in the market economy as a relatively extraordinary event—of undoubted importance to those directly regulated by its terms, but altogether dubious as a source of generalized legal principle. This attitude not only prevailed amongst leading scholars of administrative law,[3] but also was reinforced by the pronounced judicial suspicion of activist legislation. Although many statutory interventions did survive attacks on their constitutionality, the very complexity of the doctrinal analysis necessary for judicial validation emphasized the legally problematic character of the activist enterprise. While activist legislatures might find that one or another innovation had achieved judicial recognition, they could never be sure of success the next

2. My own views on this matter are close to those of Richard Hofstadter, who emphasizes the extent to which the New Deal broke from its Progressive predecessors. See his AGE OF REFORM 272–328 (1955).

3. See W. CHASE, THE AMERICAN LAW SCHOOL AND THE RISE OF ADMINISTRATIVE GOVERNMENT (1982). Scholars taking a different view, most notably Frank Goodnow and Ernst Freund, were isolated figures in legal education; despite the high quality of their writings, their work had very little impact in legal circles. See *id.* at 48–83, 123–124.

time around. It was as if each regulatory statute marked a volcanic disruption of the tumultuous but familiar sea of judge-made law. However prominent a statutory peak, it could not be treated as a fixed point in the legal landscape. At any moment, it might sink without a trace beneath the common law sea from which it had so remarkably emerged.

Given this picture of the legal world, it was plainly imprudent to look upon activist statutes as if they contained general principles that might illuminate legal disputes far removed from the particular problems they explicitly addressed. Thus, a lawyer confronting a trucking dispute in 1925 would immediately see the relevance of a common law judgment involving horse-drawn carriages rendered in 1825, but he was unlikely to consider whether the Interstate Commerce Commission had dealt with an analogous problem involving railroads in 1924.[4] However useful it was to explore each volcano, the ultimate test of a lawyer was his capacity to navigate the open sea. And the conceptual map[5] required of a lawyer who hoped to stay afloat was categorically different from the mountaineering guide required for one or another statutory prominence.

It was precisely this general sense of the prevailing legal landscape that was transformed by the New Deal. After the Supreme Court's dramatic capitulation in 1937, no competent lawyer could plausibly doubt the permanence

---

4. Indeed, he might well find a constitutional problem in subtle changes in the truck's common law status. See e.g., Smith v. Cahoon, 283 U.S. 553 (1930).

5. I explore the idea of a conceptual map in a very different context in my essay, *The Structure of Subchapter C: An Anthropological Comment*, 87 YALE L. J. 436 (1977). For more general reflections on similar ideas, see C. GEERTZ, THE INTERPRETATION OF CULTURES 87–125 (1973); M. DOUGLAS, NATURAL SYMBOLS 19–112 (1973).

of the mighty peaks that displaced particularly tumultuous areas of the open sea. Indeed, the New Deal threw up so many volcanos so quickly that it often became very hard to glimpse the sea, let alone navigate with the same old maps. Increasingly, the New Deal lawyer found himself surrounded with vast disordered heaps of legislative mandate and bureaucratic decree that displayed institutional structures and technical jargon unfamiliar to the common law. If the profession wanted to survive and prosper (and that goes without saying), it had only one choice: try to make what legal sense it could of an alien world forced upon it by political circumstances beyond its control.

The language of New Deal statute and regulation bespeaks the difficulty of taking the first awkward steps in the new world of activist legal meaning. The rhetoric of the new administrative state mixed vacuous abstraction with mindless particularity in an odd way that all of us have nonetheless learned to take for granted. Both of these rhetorical sins are, I think, attributable to the difficulty of finding one's way in an unfamiliar landscape without undue reliance upon suspect common law maps.

Begin with New Deal vacuity. Code words like "public convenience and necessity" functioned in the manner of no trespassing signs. They served to place vast areas of activist decision off limits for ordinary lawyerly conversation. Of course, the profession displayed no similar reluctance when it came to seizing control of new power positions in the burgeoning bureaucracies. Yet when lawyers talked about the aims of activist legislation within their bureaucratic boxes, the grand vacuities of New Deal statutes permitted them to declare their discursive independence from traditional legalisms. Rather than linking activist law-talk to their suspect common law inheritance, lawyer-bureaucrats legitimated their conversation through vague appeals to "expertise" or "the political process" or some other catchphrase unknown to the common law. The critical point was to make it clear that the exercise of administrative discretion need not be defended in traditional lawyerly ways, that whatever else good public policy might be, it was *not* to be confounded with common law principles.[6]

Despite their brave declarations of independence, however, the new activist lawyers did not find it easy to achieve a disciplined form of conversation within their bureaucratic power centers. While they organized small islands of talk with ideas like "good-faith bargaining," the demands of activist lawmaking far outstripped the profession's capacities for self-expression. As a consequence, countless common law-isms secreted themselves into the substance and process of the administrative state. When the prevailing discomfort with traditional rhetoric made this impossible, New Deal discourse took an even more despairing turn. With common law legalisms suspect, and new abstractions in short supply, the effort to formulate activist rules often forced lawyers to speak in language of extraordinary specificity—as if the problem of interpretation might be solved by saying *precisely* what one meant in exhaustive detail.

Such desperate efforts to particularize legal meanings, however, could not compensate for the profession's loss of confidence in its common law moorings. No matter how explicit and elaborate Section 101 (a) (ii) (B) (6) (qq) might become, interpretive difficulties would remain. In-

6. For a recent study that emphasizes this tendency and explores its historical roots, see W. CHASE, *supra* note 3.

deed, the proliferation of particularities only served to emphasize the radical character of the legal transformation initiated by the New Deal. If, after determined effort, lawyers could place an especially problematic proviso in the context of something as large as a single statute, they deserved congratulations for their heroic labors. The very notion that law was a seamless web, that no part could be viewed separate from the whole, seemed absurd pretension. Given the New Deal transformation of the legal landscape, who could say there *was* a whole, let alone what it looked like?

Despite the profession's best efforts, this sense of disorientation could not be localized within the islands of discourse directly affected by activist legislation. Not only did the search for common law precedent increasingly lead to mountains of state or federal regulation of superior legal authority; the very nature of the search underwent an important change. By the 1920s, the profession had come to view the common law as containing something more than the jumble of procedurally oriented writs familiar a century earlier. After generations of legal exploration, it had begun to seem possible to map the sea of unruly precedent with the aid of general principles of tort, contract, and the like—principles that made the particularistic categories of the historical writ system seem arbitrary and obsolete.[7] The Restatement movement of the 1920s, moreover, placed this generalizing approach to common law on a new institutional foundation, with academy, bar, and bench engaged in the mapmaking business on a grand

7. See, e.g., G. E. WHITE, TORT LAW IN AMERICA 8–12 (1980). For more skeptical views, see L. FRIEDMAN, HISTORY OF AMERICAN LAW 354–357 (1973); G. GILMORE, THE DEATH OF CONTRACT 3–54 (1974); GILMORE, THE AGES OF AMERICAN LAW 41–67 (1977).

scale.[8] Then, just as the institutional conditions seemed congenial, the shock of the activist state forced a change in discursive direction. In field after field, the emphasis was on taking apart the common law principles that had been built up with such great effort, on their deconstruction into a host of incompatibilities whose decisional weight could be appreciated only within the narrow limits of particular cases.[9]

Indeed, the very effort to map the common law became an object of Realist ridicule.[10] For some extremists, the desire for a map was itself a symptom of personal immaturity, not the beginning of professional wisdom. In one way or another, mature lawyers had to find the strength to rid themselves of the grand illusion that somebody-up-there could make some larger legal sense of the particular dispute raging about them. Rather than yearning for the ultimate Restatement, lawyers had to have the courage to find their own bearings amidst the storm of bitter discontent generated by every lawsuit.

These Realistic sensibilities have, by now, been assimilated by all lawyers—though, of course, some attempt to

8. See, e.g., Goodrich, *Story of the American Law Institute*, Wash. U. L. Q. 283–292 (1951); Yntema, *The American Law Institute*, in Legal Essays in Tribute to Orrin Kip McMurray 657 (M. Radin & A. M. Kidd, eds. 1935).

9. The marked change in direction is evidenced in the changing character of Restatements prepared over the course of the last half-century. By now, almost every important common law field has undergone two Restatements—one typically prepared before, one after, the Second World War. The second Restatement, without exception, is far more disaggregated than its prewar predecessor. For another view of the same tendency, see Kennedy, *Form and Substance in Private Law Adjudication*, 89 Harv. L. Rev. 1685, 1725–1737 (1976).

10. I comment on this tendency at greater length in my belated book review of Jerome Frank's *Law and the Modern Mind*, Daedalus 119 (Winter 1974).

suppress them and reassert the possibility of finding *the* correct doctrinal answer, while others glory in their post-Realist freedom to intuit their way to justice.[11] However different the assertive doctrinalist may appear from the romantic intuitionist, they seem to me to share a common, and mistaken, diagnosis of our Realist inheritance. Each takes Realist iconoclasm at face value and merely disagrees on whether it is the ultimate threat or the ultimate salvation. In contrast to both, I should like to advance a third interpretation. Rather than undermining the hold traditional legalisms have had on the profession, Realism was in fact a culturally conservative movement. Indeed, it was only by assimilating large chunks of Realist wisdom that the profession managed to preserve so much of its traditional common law discourse.

To see my point, imagine that our legal culture had somehow resisted the enticements of Realistic disaggregation and had vigorously adapted the Restatement approach to the new legal conditions prevailing after the New Deal. In invoking this possibility, I do not want you to imagine Restaters of the reactionary sort, intent upon preserving the purity of their understanding of the common law at any price. Instead, I wish to hypothesize a more adaptive group, one that hoped to incorporate the general lessons of the New Deal into a new synthetic understanding of the general principles informing American law.[12] From this

11. Compare R. DWORKIN, TAKING RIGHTS SERIOUSLY 279–290 (1977) and Dworkin, *No Right Answer?* in LAW, MORALITY, & SOCIETY (P. M. S. Hacker & J. Raz eds. 1977), with Kennedy, *Form and Substance, supra* note 9, and Kennedy, *Legal Formality*, 2 J. LEG. STUD. 351 (1973).

12. Since the Second World War, the American Law Institute has indeed expanded its concerns beyond the Restatement of judge-made law to the formulation of model statutes and bureaucratic guidelines, with the most notable achievements occurring in the area of criminal

perspective, it would be plain at once that an adequate synthesis could no longer be achieved within the framework of traditional generalizing methods. Before the New Deal, it was common for Restaters to suppose that they might organize the profession's talk of contract, property, and tort without paying very much attention to the swirl of legislative and bureaucratic activity surrounding their precious common law. Such a narrow approach was increasingly untenable, however, to thoughtful generalizers of the 1930s.[13] At the very most, the common law was now only one branch of a trinitarian legal system, in which statutory enactment and bureaucratic practice also served as constitutionally legitimate sources of general principle. No longer, then, could generalizers hope to extract a legal principle from judge-made law without giving close attention to the contrary voices heard from legislators and bureaucrats. Only then could they begin to locate the proper meaning and weight of common law principle against its transforming New Deal background.

Yet to say this was to say something very radical indeed for a profession that remained deeply enmeshed in its common law heritage. Before lawyers could even begin to use statutory and bureaucratic materials as sources of

---

law. For a revealing discussion, see Wechsler, *The Challenge of A Model Penal Code*, 65 Harv. L. Rev. 1097 (1952). For reasons worthy of more serious investigation, the Institute has not been at the center of the Constructive legal movement described in this book.

13. While Roscoe Pound raised an eloquent voice against common law narrowness as early as his *Common Law and Legislation*, 21 Harv. L. Rev. 383 (1908), this essay very much adopts the tone of the prophet crying in the wilderness. In contrast, similar statements of the 1930s are made with a new sense of inevitable, if far-distant, victory. See e.g., J. M. Landis, *Statutes and the Sources of Law*, in Harvard Essays Written in Honor of and Presented to Jospeh Henry Beale and Samuel Williston 213 (1934); Stone, *The Common Law in the United States*, 50 Harv. L. Rev. 4 (1936).

generalizing legal principle, they would have to invest enormous energy arguing out the concrete meanings of the new lawstuff heaped upon them. Only very gradually could the profession begin to gain the intellectual self-confidence required to elaborate middle-level principles that might begin to make a larger sense of the legislative fiat and bureaucratic practice that so commanded the new legal scene. Until such middle-level abstractions were generally available for use in the legal culture, the generalizing approach to American law would require an extraordinary leap into the unknown. The profession would be obliged to adopt wholesale a host of unfamiliar principles and methods in a desperate effort to relate common law and New Deal in a way that an adequate synthesis would require. Rather than a Restatement of familiar patterns of legal discourse, such a collective effort at legal synthesis would yield only some unfamiliar newspeak unrooted in the daily talk of everyday legal practice. Who could say what discursive disaster might come from such a radical reorientation?

In contrast, the Realist's view of the common law offered an altogether happier prospect. On his account, the cure for the profession's prevailing malaise was not self-conscious struggle with the abstract relationship between the legal principles inspiring common law and New Deal. Instead, relief would come only with the recognition that the lawyers' common law was far more complex and subtle than the common law abstractions bandied about in political talk. Rather than losing themselves in a fog of abstract political rhetoric about contract, property, and the like, the aim of legal craftsmen was to pierce the emptiness of such rhetoric. The so-called organizing concepts of the common law should be recognized as empty boxes concealing a host of distinct fact situations that required a sensitive response by Realisic lawyers with situation sense. Insofar as generalizations made sense, they would have to be built up painfully case-by-case; the result would be a body of common law doctrine far more complex and perceptive than anything a Restater could imagine.[14]

Whatever its ultimate merit, the professional response to this message should be predictable. While certain nihilistic implications of Realism would be rejected or ignored, the basic response could only be one of profoundest relief. Considered as a profession, lawyers continued to live in a social world in which clients made and broke contracts; formed and looted corporations; damaged each others' property in all the familiar ways. No less important, laymen continued to believe that it paid to hire lawyers when

14. Obviously this single paragraph cannot capture the views advanced by the very different writers who have been characterized as Realists. For an overview, see W. Rumble, American Legal Realism (1968). A good place to begin a deeper study is W. Twining, Karl Llewellyn and the Realist Movement (1973). While this intellectual biography is conceived against a broad background, its focus on Llewellyn inevitably provides a partial view of the Realist movement as a whole. In particular, Llewellyn did not play a significant role in the effort by some Realists to engage in a quantitative form of empirical social science, an effort that is undoubtedly an indirect ancestor of the Constructive fact-finding enterprise I will be considering in Chapter 4. For a complex set of reasons, however, this Realist invocation of social science never went much beyond the pronunciamento stage. See Schlegel, *American Legal Realism and Empirical Social Science: From the Yale Experience*, 28 Buffalo L. Rev. 459 (1979). It did not serve to induce legal educators, let alone the profession at large, to cultivate the skills necessary for disciplined empirical analysis.

The particularizing tendency I am emphasizing in the text, in contrast, did have a pervasive professional impact. Some early examples are provided in essays by Oliphant, *A Return to Stare Decisis*, 14 Am. Bar Ass'n. J. 71, 159 (1928); Radin, *The Theory of Judicial Decision or How Judges Think*, 11 Am. Bar Ass'n. J. 357 (1925), as well as much better-known works by J. Frank, Law and the Modern Mind (1930) and K. Llewellyn, The Bramble Bush (1960).

the verbal going got tough. Within this context, it would not do for the profession to transform each common law case into a vain effort to answer the Restater's question about the meaning of it all. What was desperately required was a method by which one might *continue* talking in largely traditional ways about particular disputes without raising the large abstractions that had gotten the common law into such political troubles. It was precisely this that Realism could promise the profession. Its skepticism about legal abstraction permitted lawyers to proceed in good conscience with infinite variations on traditional forms of professional talk, despite the larger legitimacy crisis that this very discourse had provoked. So long as one could talk about particular contracts without paying explicit fealty to the ideal of Free Contract, property, without Private Property, fault, without Fault, the profession might survive the political crisis with its basic discursive equipment intact. Realistic lawyering, in short, provided the professional community with a credible means of insulating the established universe of legal meanings from the political crisis in which it had been implicated.

Not that the received view of the Realists as iconoclast-reformers is altogether mistaken. Indeed, iconoclasm was an indispensable part of the process by which the New Deal generation liberated itself from its predecessors. In the 1930s, after all, an interpretation of the common law that emphasized its roots in Free Contract and Private Property was not merely one possible form of legal understanding; it was the *only* living example of a comprehensive approach to legal analysis. Before a new form of legal generalization could appear plausible, the profession had to be thoroughly convinced that familiar generalizations about "the" common law were no longer legally acceptable. Realist iconoclasm, however exaggerated, played an important part in this process.

By discrediting the old synthesis, moreover, the Realist-reformer also made it easier for lawyers to revise common law doctrines on a piecemeal basis in ways that might accommodate half-formed intuitions about the meaning of the new regime ushered in by the New Deal. Since traditional doctrines were now demoted to the status of working rules of thumb, it became easier to supplement, modify, and transform them whenever a Realistic sense of situational justice required it. Thus the consideration doctrine came to sit, however uncomfortably, with new ideas of unconscionability; negligence, with strict liability. The multiplication of such dissonances was an occasion not for anxiety but for the proud recognition of the capacity of the common law, under Realistic leadership, to adapt pragmatically to the political repudiation of its laissez-faire past. The emerging pattern of common law discourse came, in short, to resemble the new administrative discourse that had overwhelmed it.[15] In both public and private domains, lawyers would learn to look upon organizing abstractions—be they "contract" or "the public convenience and necessity"—with deep skepticism. The life of the law was to be found in the sensitive formation of highly particularistic rules, and in the Realistic refusal to general-

---

15.    There is a good deal of historical irony, then, in the fact that it was Roscoe Pound's critique of the "work of the on-coming generation of American law teachers," *The Call for a Realist Jurisprudence*, 44 HARV. L. REV. 697 (1931), that contributed to the Realists' sense of themselves as a distinct legal movement. For it was Pound's own sociological jurisprudence that played an important role in legitimating the pervasive skepticism about legal abstractions characteristic of the prevailing discourse in modern administrative law. See W. CHASE, *supra* note 3, at 109 (1982).

ize those rules beyond the particular contexts that gave them meaning.

To summarize: no group of professionals can survive economically, sociologically, spiritually without a general sense that it provides a distinctive service of value. Since attorneys are essentially hired talkers, they could hardly allow themselves—not to mention others—believe that they had been reduced to speechlessness by the New Deal's constitutionally successful challenge to their laissez-faire intellectual heritage. Yet the very pervasiveness of the traditional legal culture made a clear break professionally unthinkable. Like it or not, the common law was the only law that lawyers really knew how to handle; and the profession could hardly afford to keep clients waiting while it conducted a generation-long seminar on the relationship between its traditional talk and the new legal premises generated by the emerging legislative and bureaucratic political order. The challenge, instead, was to keep on talking in familiar ways while somehow recognizing that something important had happened. It is precisely this that Realism provided the profession. On the one hand, the Realistic lawyers' *skepticism about abstraction* permitted them to keep invoking particular doctrines inherited from the past without confronting their foundation in laissez-faire legal theory. On the other hand, their *confidence in intuitionistic adaptation* of received doctrine in the light of vaguely formulated public policies permitted them to assure themselves, as well as others, that American lawyers had recognized that the American people were insisting on a New Deal. It is this intuitionistic effort to craft legal rules to fit very particularized fact-patterns that marks the Realist heritage, as I shall define it, in both administrative law and common law.

It is also precisely this heritage that the profession is, and should be, outgrowing as it looks back upon the New Deal at half-century. I hope to persuade you that it is not Realism but Constructivism that will permit us to confront, if not resolve, the basic legal challenges posed by our present form of political and social life. In contrast to the Realists' efforts to grasp each particular dispute in its infinite particularity, Constructive lawyers emphasize the danger of exaggerating the legal importance of the idiosyncratic. They call instead for a "statement of the facts" that relates individual conflicts to the systematic structural tensions of social life. In contrast to the Realists' efforts at intuitionistic adaptation of laissez-faire traditions, Constructive lawyers fear that muddled efforts to improve upon the invisible hand will yield a world even less just and humane than free-market capitalism. They call instead for the systematic test of particular activist interventions by legal principles that seek to capture the basic ideals that have led the American people to embrace activism in the first place.

Nor should it be thought remarkable that it has taken fifty years for the Constructive challenge to reach professional maturity. As we have seen, it is one thing to call for a systematic way of describing systemic facts and arguing activist values; it is quite another for a professional community to construct, out of a host of more particular insights, an ongoing conversation about the pursuit of activist values in an incredibly complex world. The intrinsic difficulty of this collective project does not, however, fully account for the delay in the rise of Constructive lawyering to professional prominence. In an awe-ful way, the rise of Constructivism required the death of the legal generation who viewed the birth of the American activist state. For these witnesses would always remember the time when activism was a legally controversial principle; for them, the return of laissez faire was not an idle speculation but a powerful psychological threat, supported by countless concrete recollections of close calls and fortuitous victories. These inevitable anxieties of a first legal generation, moreover, were best expressed by a Realist sensibility. On the one hand, the Realist rejection of laissez-faire conceptualism signaled explicit acceptance of the New Deal's repudiation of the old order; on the other hand, the Realist's failure to construct a new form of legal discourse expressed an anxious recognition that the ancien régime might not be quite the has-been it was said to be, and that if laissez faire did return, lawyers had better be prepared to take up the old ways of talking with renewed conviction.

Slowly, almost imperceptibly, the fact of individual death transforms the character of professional anxieties that fuel the Realistic adaptation to the activist state. Despite their parents' dramatic bedside stories about the evils of the ancien régime, the children of the law can only imagine the past that was their elders' living present. Soon enough, the children come to outnumber the parents, until, fifty years onward, the rise of the activist state has become just another part of the morality play that lawyers congenitally mistake for history. Nowadays, it seems obvious to all well-trained lawyers that the Old Court was wrong in contesting the constitutional legitimacy of the New Deal, that its precipitous retreat before Roosevelt in 1937 served, at best, as belated expiation for its half-century of sinful opposition to the triumphant activist state. The laissez-faire era increasingly seems a closed chapter of legal history, disconnected from the realities of present-day legal experience. Although no sane person would deny that Americans of the year 2000 might return to a world where the federal government no longer attempts to provide social security or racial justice or environmental protection, or withholds large chunks of money from our weekly paychecks, the prospect of a renewed embrace of the invisible hand is, for us, merely one of countless possibilities. It does not provoke the anxiety so often lurking beneath the surface of the emphatic activism of our immediate predecessors.[16]

The end of this particular legal anxiety, however, only serves to breed another. As a consequence of a half-century's Realist adaptation, the second activist generation finds it impossible to locate any area of legal doctrine that is not permeated with loose talk of "public policy," "unconscionability," "unequal bargaining power," and the like. The undeveloped analysis that so often follows such invocations, moreover, does not in any way detract from the seriousness with which they are professed, or the extent to which they are taken into account in shaping our public and private law. Indeed, it is this very gap between high legal purpose and low legal analysis that generates the distinctive anxieties which fuel the Constructive enterprise. When they speak so resonantly of "public policy," do lawyers have the slightest idea what they're talking about? Will the legal steps they endorse further, rather than frustrate, the activist ideals they profess? Is it not time to move beyond Realist slogans and do the hard analytic work required if we are to use law to make good its activist promise—and help our fellow citizens build a world that is more just and more free than one ruled by the invisible hand?

16.  Instead of dreaming about the return of Calvin Coolidge, *our* nightmares tend to focus upon the possibility that the activist state will end in nuclear annihilation.

# · 3 ·
# From Realism
# to Reconstruction

---

WHAT, THEN, must legal discourse look like if it is to do justice to the distinctive concerns of an activist polity?

To answer this question, we first require a clearer conception of the limited kinds of legal argument possible in a polity untainted by activist ideas. For euphony, I will call such a place the purely *reactive* state. Having established a conceptual baseline, we can then systematically investigate the conversational consequences of repudiating reactive political premises and replacing them with activist political principles. Once the abstract characteristics of activist law-talk are identified, we can begin to approach the more prominent Constructions of the past generation. This will set the stage for a more detailed inspection, in succeeding chapters, of the energetic and chaotic work at reconstruction now proceeding apace.

To forestall predictable misunderstanding, I must emphasize that my reactive and activist models are not to be read as pop-historical cartoons of the American legal past. There has never been, nor will there ever be, a time in American history when all legal conversation can be organized within a single discursive model.[1] The point of the models is not to serve as bits of bad history, but to alert us to a present possibility: that the activist dimension of our legal discourse has, fifty years after the New Deal, reached a critical stage in its practical importance and theoretical development. Rather than looking upon the ongoing Constructive enterprise with bemused detachment or outraged contempt, the thoughtful lawyer must recognize the development of a new language of power as a central professional enterprise.

## Reactive Lawyering

Imagine what the practice of law would look like in a purely reactive state. In such a hypothetical polity, the military, economic, and social foundations of daily life are not conceived as raising questions for self-conscious and systematic political decision. Instead, arrangements generated by the invisible hand are allowed to govern such matters. Military defense is left to the oceans, economic welfare to the market place, social justice to whatever-emerges-from-the-millions-of-free-decisions-made-each-day-by-countless-Americans.

For the present, I am entirely uninterested in exploring

1. For a more extensive discussion of the different uses of discursive models, see Ackerman, *Four Questions for Legal Theory*, in Nomos XXII, Property 351 (J. R. Pennock & J. W. Chapman, eds. 1980).

the (de-) merits of these (familiar) views. Instead, my aim is to emphasize the way the reactive state's systematic political allegiance to the invisible hand constrains the conversational moves open to lawyers trying to translate the grievances of their clients into legally persuasive arguments. On this level, the implications are obvious enough. Legal argument is restricted by something I shall call the *reactive constraint:* No legal argument will be acceptable if it requires the lawyer to question the legitimacy of the military, economic, and social arrangements generated by the invisible hand.

Although this conversational constraint is of a purely negative kind, it gives a definite shape to the reactive professional culture. While the constraint forbids lawyers from questioning the invisible hand, the reactive state imposes no similar bar upon lawyerly efforts to glorify the social expectations generated by existing social practices. Imagine, say, that our reactive lawyer lives in a society whose inhabitants are thoroughly socialized into the practice of keeping promises. While the reactive constraint bars advocates from questioning the efficiency and/or justice of this institutionalized practice, nothing prevents them from making it the operational premise of an affirmative legal argument. Thus, if it serves the client's interest, a lawyer is free to go into court to uphold the sanctity of keeping promises; the defendant's attorney, in turn, may be relied upon to argue that his antagonist has mistaken the prevailing practice of promise-keeping as it applies to the case. Either his client never made a binding promise in the first place, or his avoidance activity falls within one of the excuses or justifications well recognized in established practice. So the argument proceeds, each reactive lawyer attempting to provide an interpretation of institutionalized expectations that makes his client's actions seem appropriate, his antagonist's deviant.

Now there are several features of this conversational exchange that may be usefully emphasized. First, the legal conversation deals with the appraisal of particular actions against the background of ongoing social practice; thanks to the reactive constraint, the legitimacy of an entire practice is never open to legal question. Of course, prevailing practice may change over time, and so the appraisal of particular actions may change as well, but these slow changes in social practice are conceived by the legal disputants as exogenous to the self-conscious decisions made within the legal culture. So far as lawyers are concerned, the only thing worth talking about is the particular trouble generated by the actions of particular people at a particular time. The cumulative impact of these decisions upon the ebb and flow of institutional life is something that no reactive lawyer would discuss in a professionally disciplined fashion before a legally authoritative tribunal.

This leads directly to a second defining feature. So far as the law is concerned, the only decisive question is whether the challenged action deviates from institutionalized norms. Each lawyer tries to provide a persuasive account of ongoing practice that makes the opponent's conduct appear deviant, his own client's behavior innocent or justifiable or, at the very least, excusable.

Given this focus on the deviance of particular actions, it follows, third, that the original disputants are typically in the best position to develop the facts and values relevant to a just decision. Their particular actions, after all, generated the dispute in the first place, and so they should be in a good position to organize the presentation of relevant evidence. Similarly, lawyers representing both sides are, as well-socialized citizens, familiar with the prevailing social practices that serve as the source of governing norms. While opposing advocates will, of course, interpret established expectations in a way that puts their client's actions in the most favorable light, reactive decisionmakers have no reason to expect that advocates will ignore any factors relevant to a mature appraisal of deviance.

Indeed, under proper guidance from an official, there is no reason why a jury of laymen cannot make the ultimate decision about deviance. So it is the jury trial that represents the paradigmatic example of popular participation in, and control over, the legal system. In contrast, even a popularly responsive legislature is viewed with suspicion.[2] No system of legislative rules can hope to reflect the complex web of principles well-socialized people use to elaborate the structure of institutionalized expectation. The very effort at codification bespeaks intellectual arrogance. Why try to lay down rules when a jury of laymen can deploy their subtle sense of the situation in an individualized appraisal? Moreover, even a relatively successful code will soon become obsolete as expectations evolve under the benign guidance of the invisible hand. The mere fact that the legislature is democratically elected should not permit it to go on arrogant and unwise lawmaking escapades. For the jury is also a democratic institution, and it is better adapted to handle the central problems of reactive lawmaking. Rather than framing comprehensive codes, legislators should be modest in their ambitions, addressing discrete and limited problems that somehow escape the ken of the case-oriented jury. Call this fourth feature of the

2. For a particularly extreme statement, see J. GRAY, THE NATURE AND SOURCES OF THE LAW 170–173 (rev. ed. 1921).

reactive model the dominance of lay adjudication over popular legislation.

Finally, while the effort to define deviance may involve a host of complex contextual arguments, the legal conversation will have a natural end. There is only so much that can be said about particular actions before the conversation gets repetitive. The only thing left to do is for the jury to engage in a densely textured judgment upon the defendant's conduct—either it was deviant or it wasn't. If it was, the defendant should set things right; if not, not. Next case.

## Activist Lawyering

Now assume that, for one reason or another, the dominant opinion amongst the citizenry no longer holds that the country's military, economic, and social problems can take care of themselves without self-conscious tending. Assume, further, that the citizenry insists that law and lawyers have a central role to play in activist governance, and consider how these simple points will transform the profession's conversational repertoire.

Most obviously, the subject of legal conversation will no longer be limited to the appraisal of individual actions against the background of presumptively legitimate social practice. At least some of the time, the ongoing practice itself will be the source of the legal problem. To put the point in paradox: while the reactive lawyer is exclusively concerned with determining individual deviance, the activist lawyer is also concerned with identifying actions that seem innocent but require modification if the entire practice is to function in a politically acceptable fashion. What could be more innocent than a society at peace, happily minding its own business—except when a hostile enemy threatens? What could be more innocent than selling a good at a price the buyer is willing to pay—except when free markets, left unregulated, generate systematically inefficient and unjust results? What could be more innocent than flushing a toilet—except when a billion daily flushes destroy a precious ecosystem?

Such problems require a radical revision in the profession's conversational repertoire. First, the activist lawyer will require a new way of describing the relevant facts. It would be incredibly time-consuming, for example, to describe the practice of driving an automobile by reporting that Roe drove from *A* to *B*, Doe drove from *C* to *D*, and so on. It would also miss the point of activist concern, which is to assess the extent to which the practice, considered as a whole, requires self-conscious legal regulation to operate in an acceptable fashion. Given this concern, individualized descriptions seem nothing more than a series of anecdotes. What is required instead is something I shall call a *structural* account—a statement of the facts that reveals the ways an activity might be feasibly reorganized to avoid or ameliorate the inefficiencies and injustices it may be generating. If lawyers are successful in producing such an account, moreover, their very triumph will serve to push them even deeper into the structural enterprise. For it will quickly become obvious that the regulation of one activity—say driving a car—will have an important impact on the way other activities—walking, breathing, and the like—are organized. Should lawyers not, then, try to understand these important "second-order effects" by imbedding the initial description into a more comprehensive structural account?

This quest for ever-broader empirical understanding must, of course, be kept under reasonable control in practical law-craft, lest it delay necessary decisions in a continually expanding and pointlessly expensive fact-finding spiral. In principle, however, the activist lawyer has no objection to the selective investigation of second-order effects—and is likely to develop all sorts of lore defining the occasions, and institutional contexts, in which such explorations are worthwhile. In contrast, the very notion of a disciplined assessment of second-order effects does not fit within the reactive lawyer's frame of reference. The point here is to do justice to the very particular facts of the dispute demanding resolution, rather than waste precious time on idle speculation. If a series of particular decisions yields untoward results, there will be time enough to consider the problem whenever "any visible inconvenience doth appear."[3]

From an activist perspective, this cavalier attitude toward the future does not merely generate avoidable hardship; its self-confident assertion of future reactive prowess is often unjustified. Given the high costs of litigation and legislative lobbying, many systemic "inconveniences" may never appear in a way that is "visible" to reactive decision-makers because the injured parties lack the money, energy, and organizational incentives to force their grievances onto the reactive agenda.[4] The refusal to inter-

    3. The dictum is from Lord Nottingham's judgment in the *Duke of Norfolk's Case*, 3 Ch. Cases 49 (1682). Despite the antique diction, Lord Nottingham very much remains a conversational presence amongst today's lawyers.
    4. See, e.g., Galanter, *Why the "Haves" Come Out Ahead: Speculations on the Limits of Legal Change*, 9 LAW & SOC. REV. 95 (1974); Cooter & Kornhauser, *Can Litigation Improve the Law Without the Help of Judges?* 9 J. LEG. STUD. 139 (1980); Priest, *Selective Characteristics of Litigation*, 9 J. LEG. STUD. 399 (1980).

pret particular facts within their social and economic context seems guaranteed, in the end, to achieve only one objective: to blind the reactive lawyer to the very existence of the systemic failures that motivate activist concerns.

The activist's structural statement of the facts, moreover, serves as a prologue to a continuing disagreement over the proper shape of legal conversation. Having rejected the reactive preoccupation with the elaborate description of particular actions, the activist is now in a position to challenge a second defining feature of the reactive model: its concern with the extent to which challenged actions offend institutionalized expectations. The reactive lawyer's search for individual deviance will begin to seem patently myopic, often leading to a pernicious kind of scapegoating in which an individual actor is wrongly held responsible for the inadequate workings of the invisible hand. The proper place to begin the normative argument is not with assertions of individual deviance, but with the reasons the existing practice, taken as a whole, may be considered inefficient or unjust. Once viewed in this systemic way, it will rarely seem plausible to see an entire practice as deviant. Driving a car, for example, *does* make breathing and walking more difficult, but this doesn't suggest that we should all walk to work; market exchange may well exacerbate many kinds of social injustice, but this hardly implies the suppression of all markets everywhere. Instead, the activist legal task is to design a better form of accommodation between competing activities than the one thrown up by the invisible hand.

Yet, if they are to hope for a reasoned effort at such an accommodation, activist lawyers will have to deal with values far more abstractly than their reactive counterparts. Rather than appraising individual actions against the background of concrete social practice, they must learn to assess the extent to which concrete practice conforms to the social ideals affirmed by prevailing activist legal principles. For reactive advocates, in contrast, such an abstract normative inquiry forces lawyers beyond their proper role into the vagaries of social engineering and is fated to tragic failure.

It is a serious mistake, however, to take reactive prophecies of doom at face value. While an explicit concern with the legitimacy of entire social practices does set activist lawyers apart, it does not commit them to call for an ever-deeper penetration by government officials into ongoing social life. Insofar as they live in a *liberal* activist state, activist lawyers will be constantly emphasizing the risk that heavy-handed intervention can become counterproductive or illegitimate or both. In addition, an ongoing concern with deregulation will seem a vital component of the activist enterprise: it is only by eliminating misbegotten or obsolescent initiatives that we may project the polity's energies into those areas where focused intervention will enhance, rather than diminish, the exercise of individual rights and the quality of collective life. Activist legal discourse, in short, is entirely consistent with a strong commitment to limited government. Indeed, so far as the activist is concerned, it provides the best way of assuring that government's limited energies will not be exhausted in wrongheaded scapegoating and empty gestures.

The new kinds of structural description and evaluation challenge, in turn, the third feature of the reactive model: parties to particular disputes can no longer be relied upon to present all the relevant facts, articulate all the relevant values. Their particular controversy may be atypical and create a misleading impression of the problems experienced by most participants in the practice under scrutiny. It follows that the particular arguments advanced by the primary disputants may properly be complemented by others proffered by a bureaucracy concerned with the public interest or by lawyers engaged to represent those groups who would otherwise be unrepresented. Moreover, the ultimate decisionmaker will often have cause to be dissatisfied with the state of the record tendered to him, some critical dimension of the dispute having been ignored by the parties who happen to be participating in the decision. In such a case, the activist decisionmaker may well be given the right to express dissatisfaction in a way that would surprise his reactive counterpart. He might, for example, be allowed to go beyond the record to take notice of important data or force the parties to respond to issues they have ignored. Litigation is no longer conceived as a bipolar dispute about deviance controlled by a small number of private parties. The activist lawsuit is, in principle, expandable into a polycentric dispute[5] in which the decisionmaker may take an affirmative role in defining the relevant facts and values the parties are to explore.

Within this context, the primacy of lay adjudication falls under a cloud. At the very least, untrained jurors cannot be trusted to detect the occasions on which the parties have ignored critical dimensions of the necessary struc-

5. I owe the term, and much else besides, to Lon Fuller's seminal essay, *The Forms and Limits of Adjudication*, 92 HARV. L. REV. 353 (1978). For more particular insights into the character of the activist judicial process, I am also greatly indebted to the work of Abram Chayes, Owen Fiss, and Martin Shapiro. See M. SHAPIRO, COURTS 1–64 (1981); Chayes, *The Supreme Court 1981 Term—Foreword: Public Law Litigation and the Burger Court*, 96 HARV. L. REV. 4 (1982); Fiss, *The Supreme Court 1978 Term—Foreword: The Forms of Justice*, 93 HARV. L. REV. 1 (1979); Chayes, *The Role of the Judge in Public Law Litigation*, 89 HARV. L. REV. 1281 (1976).

tural description. If they are not to be displaced by expert fact-finders, it is only because of other (abstract) values that justify their continuing participation in legal decision-making. Most notably, the case for jury involvement will increasingly be seen to rest upon its capacity to check the tyrannical abuse of official power by an overweening bureaucracy.[6] Even here, however, lay adjudication will not be endowed with quite the same paradigmatic significance it commands within the reactive interpretation of the legal world. Rather than glorifying jury trial, the activist lawyer will look to the legislature as the preeminent forum for the expression of the popular will. This is where the People speak, through their politically responsible agents, about the best ways to revise existing social practices. It is the lawyer's task to incorporate these new messages into the ongoing scheme of activist governance, as well as to alert the People to basic issues arising from practice that seem to require their focused attention. The fourth feature of our activist model, then, emphasizes the democratic primacy of popular legislation over lay adjudication. The lawyer's ultimate appeal is no longer to a random audience of twelve laymen, but to a carefully selected group of full-time political representatives, aided by a proliferating group of professionally trained assistants.

It should be plain, fifth, that this kind of legal conversation has no end. The People must be constantly apprised of new tensions arising in the activist effort to govern an immense variety of competing activities. Indeed, the questions of principle and policy raised by activist governance

---

6. Cf. M. KADISH & S. KADISH, DISCRETION TO DISOBEY (1973). In addition to its potential as a check against bureaucratic tyranny, the jury may also discharge many other useful functions in an activist state. For a particularly insightful account, see G. CALABRESI & P. BOBBIT, TRAGIC CHOICES 57–72 (1978).

overwhelm the time and energy of the small number of elected representatives who speak in the People's name. The lawmaking functions of administrative agencies no longer seem a peripheral matter; instead, the quality of decisionmaking in these institutions is a prime question of legal concern.[7] Not only is there a deepening interest in the way statutes (fail to) shape bureaucratic incentives; there is also a demand for review procedures that can reliably test bureaucratic actions to assure that structural fact-finding and agency lawmaking proceed in accord with activist legal principle.

While these review proceedings may be channeled into specialized new tribunals or remitted to more traditional courts, they will everywhere tend to erode principles of finality familiar to reactive lawyers. Although reactive lawsuits come to a natural end when deviants are forced to repay their debts to those they have aggrieved, the activist lawsuit is but a chapter in a never-ending story of the polity's struggle with an ongoing problem. Particular chapter endings will, of course, have a special importance for particular litigants, who may walk away from their lawsuit with a final judgment on their particular dispute. Even these final judgments may be reopened, however, with an ease that would surprise a reactive lawyer. For it is always possible that the abstract values served by finality may be outweighed, in a particular case, by changing structural facts and emerging activist values. A final judgment no longer suggests that everything worth saying has been said, only that it is best, all things considered, to say no more for a time.

Yet, while the unending work of structural appraisal

7. See P. SCHUCK, SUING GOVERNMENT (1983); Stewart, *The Reformation of American Administrative Law*, 88 HARV. L. REV. 1667 (1975).

and reappraisal is going on, citizens must face up to the fact that they each have one life to live. Unless they choose the path of revolution, they must conform their conduct to the expectations generated by existing social institutions, however much they may hope to change them. This perception, in turn, motivates the last element of my model of activist discourse. It allows us to find a new place for the traditional skills and modalities of reactive lawyering. Although activist citizens no longer look upon social institutions as the natural consequences of the invisible hand, they believe that they often have a right to rely upon the expectations generated by social practices unless and until they are revised through legal process. Thus, when somebody violates existing expectations, the injured party will often see a point in hiring a lawyer to charge the adversary with a wrongful deviation from an established practice in the familiar reactive manner.

Nonetheless, the rise of the activist state potentially transforms the nature of the humblest suit in tort, property, or contract. Although, in a purely reactive state, the only question these lawsuits explicitly raise is the extent to which one side or the other deviated from expectations fairly derived from ongoing practice, the fall of the reactive constraint makes it possible for either side to attempt a new conversational turn. Rather than justifying a claim in terms of existing practice, a lawyer may seek to persuade the court that existing practice does not deserve state support in the light of the law's ongoing pursuit of structural justice. To take a stark case: southern blacks of the 1950s did not deny that they were expected to sit in segregated railways and buses. They sought to challenge existing practice as unconstitutional, and the mere fact that they were defending a common law trespass action did not seem to them sufficient reason to defer their challenge.

This does not imply, of course, that the activist state will allow private lawsuits to be transformed in activist ways whenever a party tries to do so. All things considered, it may be wise to insulate the system of "private law" from many of these challenges and divert them to specialized activist institutions of structural justice. But, then again, it may seem unwise, or even fundamentally unfair, for a private party to gain legal victory by shunting the question of structural injustice into some distant activist forum. The key point here is that the question of coordinating the reactive (private) law with the system of activist (public) law will seem a question of central significance to lawyers at all levels. It could not, by definition, even arise in a purely reactive culture.

It is the centrality of this *coordination* question that constitutes the sixth, and final, feature of my model of activist legal discourse. Its resolution will characteristically be a complex business. Only one thing is clear: whenever a "private" litigant *is* allowed to raise questions of activist justice, the legal conversation in traditional law courts will be particularly tension-full, seeking somehow to mediate the five preceding features of activist legal conversation with the very different conceptions of fact (one) and value (two)—not to mention adjudication (three), democracy (four), and finality (five)—generated by a purely reactive understanding of the controversy.[8]

8. For futher reflections upon the procedural tensions involved in the coordination of active and reactive themes in a single lawsuit, see the literature inaugurated by Fuller, Chayes, and Fiss, *supra* note 5. The substantive dilemmas generated by the effort to define legitimate reliance interests while pursuing activist objectives has been at the center of my own work in property law—B. ACKERMAN, PRIVATE PROPERTY AND THE CONSTITUTION (1977), and Ackerman, *Regulating Slum Housing Markets on Behalf of the Poor: Of Housing Codes, Housing Subsidies*

## From Process to Substance

In remarking on the rise of the activist state, I hardly wish to claim any great novelty of insight. Much of the most important academic work since the last World War is not only instinct with a similar awareness but also marked by a determination to move beyond Realistic intuitionism and particularism. The most influential of these Constructive efforts was the conception of legal process advanced by Henry Hart and Albert Sacks,[9] and pursued vigorously by a host of area specialists who looked to these Harvard scholars for inspiration.[10] For this group, it was plain that the profession could no longer see itself as primarily concerned with the traditional—and reactive—aim of prepar-

---

*and Income Redistribution Policy,* 80 YALE L. J. 1093 (1971)—as well as that of many others working on the foundations of the common law in an activist polity. Compare, e.g., Kronman, *Contract Law and Distributive Justice,* 89 YALE L. J. 472 (1980), with C. FRIED, CONTRACT AS PROMISE (1981); and compare G. CALABRESI, THE COSTS OF ACCIDENTS: A LEGAL AND ECONOMIC ANALYSIS (1970), with Fletcher, *Fairness and Utility in Tort Theory,* 85 HARV. L. REV. 537 (1972). For some more general reflections on the relationship between the protection of individual rights and the pursuit of activist ideals, see R. DWORKIN, TAKING RIGHTS SERIOUSLY (1977); Wellington, *Common Law Rules and Constitutional Double Standards: Some Notes on Adjudication,* 83 YALE L. J. 221 (1973). I have also profited greatly from Meir Cohen's book, PERSONS AND ORGANIZATIONS, forthcoming from the University of California Press. See also, *infra* chap. 5, note 20.

9.   *The Legal Process: Basic Problems in the Making and Application of Law* (tentative edition: 1958)—undoubtedly the most influential unpublished work in recent legal history.

10.   See, e.g., L. JAFFE, JUDICIAL CONTROL OF ADMINISTRATIVE ACTION (1965); H. PACKER, THE LIMITS OF THE CRIMINAL SANCTION (1968); H. WELLINGTON, LABOR AND THE LEGAL PROCESS (1968). I discuss this group further in my review of Jerome Frank's *Law and the Modern Mind,* 103 DAEDALUS 119 (Winter 1974). See also White, *The Evolution of Reasoned Elaboration: Jurisprudential Criticism and Social Change,* 59 VA. L. REV. 279 (1973).

ing a case for trial and defending the jury's verdict on appeal. Instead, lawyers trained by Hart and Sacks tried to understand the way their clients' interests were mediated by the ongoing interaction between court, bureaucracy, and legislature. Within this framework, advocacy before a court was no longer exhausted by an effort to elaborate the structure of institutionalized expectations as expressed in the common law. Instead, courts were to be instructed elaborately upon their own lawmaking limitations compared with the bureaucracies and legislatures that had become such prominent bodies in the activist legal universe. Rather than reacting to particular fact-situations as if they were the primary lawmakers, the courts were first to identify those legal functions better performed by other elements in the activist lawmaking system. Indeed, this exercise of institutional coordination gave the judiciary a new lease on life. As a corps of generalists with life tenure, judges were in a unique position to understand the comparative advantages of each of the diverse lawmaking institutions of the activist state—and to help different institutions work together in a partnership for the public good.

Yet, however important this effort at reorientation, the legal process construction was plainly inadequate in two particulars. First, these scholars operated with inadequate models of the bureaucratic and legislative processes they sought to assimilate into the legal consciousness. Instead of building realistic, let alone rigorous, models of bureaucratic and legislative behavior, they were content with simplistic conceptions of these institutions. Although legal process scholars were perfectly aware that legislatures and bureaucracies made bad mistakes, these errors were treated as a series of isolated blunders, not the product of systemic failures. For each individual blunder, the job of the court was to engage the errant institution in Socratic dialogue, focusing the attention of legislators and bureaucrats on dimensions of the problem they somehow missed the first time around. The hopeful implication was that, under proper legal questioning, bureaucrats would make good their promise of expertise and legislators would redeem their claims to democratic legitimacy. The possibility of some deeper structural failing in the process of activist lawmaking was not something, apparently, that lawyers had much to say about.[11]

An even more serious flaw becomes clear when we turn from legal process to legal substance. Here, the Harvard group simply had nothing to offer, other than a vague recognition that new forms of expertise were aborning somewhere in bureaucracy-land. Moreover, when other brave scholars tried to impose order on the substance of activist law, the products of their heroic labors only confirmed the mass of lawyerdom in its Realistic predispositions. There is

11. This deficiency is slowly being corrected by recent writers in the legal process tradition. See, e.g., G. CALABRESI, A COMMON LAW FOR THE AGE OF STATUTES (1982) (legislative failure); J. ELY, DEMOCRACY AND DISTRUST (1980) (legislative failure); Chayes, *supra* note 5 (bureaucratic failure); Fiss, *supra* note 5 (bureaucratic failure). Unfortunately, these contemporary writers fail to move beyond the legal process tradition's casual treatment of legislative and bureaucratic phenomena. Thus far, there has been very little inclination to draw on analytic political science in an effort to elaborate the many different scenarios that may ultimately engender one or another breakdown in the legislative or bureaucratic process. For some pioneering efforts along these lines, see W. NISKANEN, BUREAUCRACY AND REPRESENTATIVE GOVERNMENT (1971); S. ROSE-ACKERMAN, CORRUPTION: A STUDY IN POLITICAL ECONOMY (1978); Spitzer, *Multicriteria Choice Processes: An Application of Public Choice Theory to Bakke, the F.C.C. and the Courts*, 88 YALE L. J. 717 (1979). For thoughtful reviews of the more general literature, see D.MUELLER, PUBLIC CHOICE (1979); A. K. SEN, COLLECTIVE CHOICE AND SOCIAL WELFARE (1970).

much to be said—both pro and con—about the extraordinary reconceptualization of legal discourse advanced by Harold Lasswell and Myres MacDougal in collaboration with a dedicated group of students whom they inspired in postwar New Haven.[12] The important point here, however, was the profession's refusal to engage in the argument. It was not as if the profession tested the Lasswell-MacDougal analysis and found it wanting; instead, with the notable exception of international law, the school utterly failed to establish itself as a conversational presence in ongoing professional interchange. However iconoclastic the style of particular Realists, their dismissive attitude toward doctrinal analysis was far easier for the traditional legal culture to assimilate than was an urgent call to reconstruct legal doctrine on a systematic foundation of activist legal principle. For the Realists offered the profession a face-saving way to keep on talking in the traditional manner despite the political crisis this lawyerly tradition had helped provoke, while New Haven newspeak threatened to deprive a traumatized lawyerdom of its last shred of discursive self-confidence.

It is my thesis, however, that the generation now rising to legal maturity no longer requires such a security blanket. After a half-century of intuitionistic argument over particular legal meanings, we have gained sufficient experience to begin, at long last, to talk about the substance of activist law in terms that transcend the ad hoc legal categories thrown up by particular state interventions. I hardly

12. A good summary of the Lasswell-MacDougal approach may be found in M. MacDougal, H. Lasswell, & I. Vlasic, Law and Public Order in Space 1–127 (1963). For a revealing early pronouncement, see MacDougal & Lasswell, *Legal Education and Public Policy: Professional Training in the Public Interest*, 52 Yale L. J. 203 (1943).

wish to assert that the language and history of Section 101 (a) (B) (ii) (gg) is unimportant, any more than that a good common lawyer can ever forget the facts and holding of *Hadley* v. *Baxendale*. Nonetheless, there is an increasing sense that these particularities do not exhaust the relevant legal conversation. Even more remarkably, the very same rhetorical structures invoked to organize the heaps of bureaucratic and legislative materials that surround us have been carried forward to the analysis of the common law tradition. For the first time in a long time, it is becoming possible for American lawyers, regardless of specialty, to speak to one another in a common language about legal substance as well as legal process, and thereby to recognize hidden interrelationships, deeper dilemmas.

No less significantly, this Constructive breakthrough has not been achieved in the grand manner of Lasswell and MacDougal, with some masterful synthesizer providing a synoptic vision for the rest of lawyerdom even before the work of Construction has fairly begun. Instead, the new language of power is being pieced together out of a very diverse set of insights contributed by a rather disorganized bunch of scholars and practitioners, who borrow from one another in an eclectic fashion when the needs of their particular projects seem to require it. While this pragmatic process of give-and-take is the best evidence of the dynamism of the Constructive enterprise, it does engender dangers of its own—most notably that lawyers lose sight of the deeper presuppositions that implicitly organize the sound and fury of the work of Construction proceeding all around them.

This danger is all the greater for the ease with which a key element of the new Constructivism admits of misinterpretation. I refer to the complex rhetoric called "law and economics." Instead of coming to terms with this rising movement, some have sought to dismiss it as an ideological smokescreen for a reactionary legal assault upon the American activist state—which should be resisted by all progressive lawyers everywhere. However beguiling this simple interpretation, especially when it is trumpeted as the last word in critical legal theory,[13] I hope to persuade you that it is both superficial and counterproductive. Superficial, because it is based on a failure to investigate those deeper cultural structures that critical

13. For a particularly conventional statement of critical wisdom, see Horwitz, *Law and Economics: Science or Politics?*, 8 HOFSTRA L. REV. 905 (1980); for a particularly elaborate one, see Kennedy, *Cost-Benefit Analysis of Entitlement Problems: A Critique*, 33 STAN. L. REV. 387 (1981). On one level, Kennedy's critique represents little more than a rehash of conventional welfare economics. The essay's novelty lies not so much in its analysis as in its neo-Realist motivation. It seeks to demonstrate, once again, that abstract and formal doctrinal analysis cannot yield legal certainty, that only particularistic intuition can yield insight in our activist legal system. See also Kennedy, *Form and Substance*, *supra* chap. 2, note 9, at 1751–1776, 1777–1778; Kennedy, *Legal Formality*, *supra* chap. 2, note 11.

But, alas, no critic can reach ground that is higher than the position he chooses to assault. Kennedy's critique does serious damage only to those extremists, associated with the University of Chicago, who believe that efficiency is an entirely unambiguous and obviously desirable legal value which permits a pseudomechanical identification of *the* correct legal answer in every case. See Markovits, *Duncan's Do Nots: Cost-Benefit Analysis and the Determination of Legal Entitlements*, STAN. L. REV. (forthcoming, 1983). Indeed, even when considered as a critique of a Chicago cartoon, I do not think Kennedy's demonstration gets to the heart of the matter. While Kennedy is right in thinking that the concept of efficiency may often yield an indeterminate solution to a legal problem, American lawyers have long since mastered the art of using legal principles even when they cannot be reduced to mechanical rules. See DWORKIN, *supra* note 8, chaps. 2 and 3 (1977) (distinction between rules and principles). The basic inadequacies of the Chicago approach to law and economics lie in its deemphasis of the pervasive reality of transaction costs (see Chapter 4, *infra*) and its distorted account of the fundamental values of the American legal tradition (see Chapter 5, *infra*). Rather than lampooning Chicago cartoons, the task is to build a richer construction of the American legal tradition, incorporating those—and *only* those—contributions of "law and economics" that contribute to this enterprise.

legal analysts claim to emphasize in their work of demysti-
fication. Counterproductive, because this superficial explanation will encourage the profession to disdain those
Constructive skills that are essential if the profession is to
aid in the legal achievement of the progressive values the
critics profess to champion. Rather than a hostile assault,
"law and economics" permits a vast enrichment of the
conversational resources available to lawyers trying to
make sense of the legal foundations of an activist state.

Not that I wish to deny the laissez-faire sympathies of
some leading practitioners of the new form of activist law-
talk—especially those who find inspiration in the pronun-
ciamentos issued regularly to the faithful from the University of Chicago.[14] This is hardly the first time, however,
that both true believers and critical critics have managed
to mistake the ultimate contribution of the movement they
so enthusiastically applaud and malign. While I suppose
all of us will have to endure an extended shouting match
pairing outrageous and self-congratulatory Chicagoan
against obscure and critical Ungero-Marxist,[15] I hope to

14.  Codified for easy reading in R. POSNER, ECONOMIC ANALYSIS OF
LAW (2 ed. 1977).

15.  Or, if Ungero-Marxist seems too much of a mouthful, simply
conjoin the last names of any two of the other eminences who are so
casually invoked as inspiration by a leading critic: Foucault, Gramsci,
Hegel, Levi-Strauss, Mannheim, Marcuse, Piaget, Sartre. See Kennedy,
*The Structure of Blackstone's Commentaries*, 28 BUFFALO L. REV. 209,
210 n. 2 (1979); Kennedy, *Distributive and Paternalist Motives in Contract and Tort Law, with Special References to Compulsory Terms and
Unequal Bargaining Power*, 41 MD. L. REV. 563, 564 n. 3 (1982). Although he aims to demystify his legal brethren, Kennedy has yet to confront, let alone resolve, the obvious inconsistencies in the views
expressed by his favored authors. His fellow critics, alas, only compound
confusion by indulging in name-dropping of their own. See, e.g., Frug,
*The City as a Legal Concept*, 93 HARV. L. REV. 1059, 1060–1061 n. 1
(1980) (invoking, *inter alia*, Arendt, Durkheim, Kennedy, Mannheim,
Marx, Unger, Weber).

urge the main line of conversation in a more Constructive direction. Looked upon as a distinctive form of legal rhetoric, "law and economics" is forcing lawyers to argue about facts and values in precisely the ways described in the preceding discussion of the conversational challenges posed by the shift from a reactive to an activist state.[16] Although, as in all pioneering efforts, the emerging discourse is sometimes shockingly primitive, the task is to make Constructive law-talk more sophisticated, rather than indulge in pseudocritical posturing.

16.   This view should not be confused with a more familiar idea. Here "law and economics" is treated as if it were the name of yet another group of social scientists seeking to gain a detached perspective upon the legal system from the vantage point of their social science speciality. While, Lord knows, the legal system can stand all the illumination that it can get, it is not this promise that accounts for the deep anxieties and high expectations that the movement has generated. Not even its most determined opponents object to the existence of a few devoted social scientists in the universities applying their methods to the legal system. After all, scientific investigation is what a university is all about, and there is no good reason to exempt the legal system from scrutiny. A problem arises only because both supporters and opponents rightly suspect that there is more to "law and economics" than disinterested science, that legal economics offers itself as a new language within which lawyers may discharge their central task of pleading for relief on behalf of their clients. Since it is *this* claim that accounts for the movement's controversial character, I shall not confuse matters by taking up the relatively uncontroversial arguments in favor of "law and economics" as one among many valid forms of interdisciplinary research.

# · 4 ·

# Reconstructing
# the Facts

---

To BRING the activist presuppositions of the new law-talk to light, reflect upon the parable that now serves as the initiatory rite of passage for all would-be lawyer-economists. I refer, of course, to the mock epic struggle between ranchers and farmers presented by Ronald Coase in *The Problem of Social Cost*.[1] In recurring to such well-worn pages, I do not wish to present yet another analysis of the precise conditions under which Coase's theorem is a valid part of microeconomic science. Instead, I want to view the Coase story as a model of a new form of power-talk lawyers may use to persuade decisionmaking officials of the merits of their client's cause.[2] When considered in this way, Coase

1. 3 J. LAW & ECON. 1 (1960).
2. For an approach to the Coase theorem that begins from the same starting point, see Gjerdingen, *The Coase Theorem and the Psychology of Common Law Thought*, 56 S. CAL. L. REV. 711 (1983). The evident

is doing nothing less than inviting us to transform the opening words of every legal conversation, words that inevitably shape all that comes afterward. What is at stake is a radical revision of that peroration lawyers call, with charming disingenuousness, the "statement of the facts."

## The Coasean Paradigm

To grasp the activist character of the Coasean lawyer's proposal, begin with his polar opposite. Imagine yourself a perfectly reactive lawyer faced with a paradigmatic reactive legal problem. A farmer comes into your office complaining about the neighboring rancher's unfortunate inclination to allow his cattle to eat the farmer's burgeoning crops. How would you go about developing the relevant facts?

We remain sufficiently socialized into reactive habits of thought for the answer to come easily. The place to begin is with the moment at which "the trouble" broke out in an obvious way. Here, it is the point at which the rancher's cows started chomping away at the farmer's crop. In scrutinizing the incident for useable evidence, moreover, the reactive lawyer will have a definite goal in view. Since he is (by definition) concerned with the deviance of particular actions, he will focus upon facts that might support the view that the rancher's actions weren't all that the community might fairly demand of him. In sifting these facts, the reactive lawyer will take advantage of a rich set of distinctions that ordinary people use to make sense of estab-

differences between Gjerdingen's work and my own will not, I hope, obscure the complementary character of concerns developed over years of fruitful conversation.

lished expectations. Thus, the farmer's lawyer will have a relatively easy time gaining substantial relief if he can persuade a jury that the rancher deliberately allowed his cattle to cross over his property line to munch away. In contrast, the rancher's lawyer will seek to convince the jury that the cattle crossing occurred by mistake or through unavoidable accident. The resulting "statement of the facts" will typically report events that are densely packed around the moment of obvious trouble, trailing back in time in directions made relevant by familiar notions of culpability, excuse, and justification.[3]

· *1* ·

If this much is recognized, we are now in a position to grasp the fundamental character of the Coasean reformulation. The analytic move that undercuts the reactive enterprise is the posit of "zero transaction costs"—more precisely, the assumption that both rancher and farmer were in perfect positions to predict[4] the future conse-

3.  Notions that may, in principle, be refined through the art of ordinary language philosophy exemplified by J. L. Austin's *A Plea for Excuses*, 57 Proc. of the Arist. Soc. 1 (1956).

4.  Note that the predictions imagined here are not probabilistic but deterministic in character. The parties are assumed to know the precise outcome that will in fact be generated by each of their possible courses of action, and not merely the way their behavior will affect the probability distribution of possible outcomes. The deterministic character of prediction follows immediately from the idea of zero transaction costs: after all, the only reason we settle for probabilistic prediction is the infinite cost involved in learning enough about the world to be *absolutely* certain about the future!

Understandably, the idea of perfectly deterministic predictions seems to overwhelm the idealizing capacities of the most resolute modelers amongst lawyer-economists. Even those Coaseans who tend to minimize the reality of transaction costs acknowledge the costs involved in making deterministic predictions, and typically assume that market actors use

quences of their actions at a time at which they could have made cost-minimizing adjustments in their courses of conduct.

To grasp the transforming power of this assumption, consider a hypothetical of the kind that provides a staple for reactive casebooks.[5] Imagine that the cows ate the crops because the supervising cowhand had been utterly incapacitated by a lightning bolt in a freak thunderstorm. Suppose further that immediately after the rancher drove his injured employee to the hospital, he personally rounded up the stray cattle and led them back to his own property. For a reactive lawyer defending the rancher, such a discovery would be a source of rhapsodic delight, since it would give him the best possible chance to per-

---

the standard probabilistic techniques—mean, variance, and so forth— in guessing about the future. This way of setting up the problem leads to a characteristic emphasis by lawyer-economists upon the parties' attitudes toward risk and the imperfections of insurance markets. See, e.g., A. M. POLINSKY, AN INTRODUCTION TO LAW AND ECONOMICS 51–56 (1983); K. Arrow, *Risk Perception in Psychology and Economics*, 20 ECON. INQ. 1 (1982); for a characteristic application of probabilistic analysis in tort law, see S. Shavell, *On Liability and Insurance*, 13 BELL J. ECON. 120 (1982). Even within this probabilistic framework, however, the parties are presumed to know the risk they run when engaging in an activity. Hence, they cannot be heard to complain of an accident when the risk they have self-consciously assumed *ex ante* materializes *ex post*.

5. Although I shall be ringing changes on Coase's rancher-farmer theme, I suspect that analogous points are most often made in classroom discussion of Vincent v. Lake Erie Transportation Co., 109 Minn. 456 (1910), which seems to have found a place in most leading casebooks. See M. FRANKLIN, INJURIES AND REMEDIES—CASES AND MATERIALS ON TORT LAW AND ALTERNATIVES 379 (1971); C. GREGORY, H. KALVEN, & R. EPSTEIN, CASES AND MATERIALS ON TORTS 36 (1977); R. POSNER, TORT LAW: CASES AND ECONOMIC ANALYSIS 180 (1982); W. PROSSER, J. WADE, & V. SCHWARTZ, TORTS, CASES AND MATERIALS 134 (7th ed. 1982); H. SHULMAN, F. JAMES, & O. GRAY, TORTS, CASES AND MATERIALS 47 (3rd ed. 1976).

suade the jury that the rancher should not pay substantial damages for this regrettable yet unavoidable accident.

In contrast, the Coasean would interpret these facts in a very different spirit. Although lightning bolts may be rare events, the nonexistence of transaction costs forces the Coasean to presume that the rancher has taken them into account in designing his cow-herding activities. Thus, given the absence of transaction costs, our rancher was in a perfect position, *before the lightning struck,* to have hired a second cowboy for the very purpose of controlling the cows during the period of his fallen comrade's misfortune. If, after considering the matter, the rancher decided that an extra cowboy wasn't worth the cost, he shouldn't be able to plead "unavoidable accident" when lightning strikes to the farmer's disadvantage. Instead, the destruction of the farmer's crop is the foreseeable consequence of the rancher's self-conscious decision to forgo the extra farmhand.

It is no exaggeration to say that there can be no such thing as an accident in the Coasean universe, nor any other event that might extenuate the rancher's responsibility for his cows' depredations. Regardless of its superficial appearance, each action should be treated as if it were the product of the rancher's self-conscious decision to pursue his interests at the expense of his neighbors. It follows that the painstaking reactive effort to assess the deviant character of particular actions—to distinguish the accidental from the deliberate, the excusable from the unjustifiable—is pointless within the limits of the Coasean idealization.

We have only begun to measure the full extent of the Coaseans' destabilization of reactive discourse. Not only do they propose to treat all actions as if they were the product of a consciously chosen plan, they also insist on treating all nonactions in the same way. After all, given the nonexistence of transaction costs, all actors may ponder their decisions to remain inactive as deeply as they consider their more affirmative activities. Why, then, should they gain special immunity when harm is the foreseeable consequence of their deliberate passivity?

Imagine, for example, that the farmer could show that there was nobody on his property at the time the rancher's cows came achomping, hence he was in no position to do anything to prevent the rancher's depredations at the moment trouble broke out on the surface of social life. Given this statement of the facts, it will seem obvious to reactive lawyers that it is the rancher's cows that caused the harm, and that, prima facie, it is the rancher who ought to be held responsible for his cows' actions.[6] In contrast, the lawyer-economist will think that this kind of causal talk obscures a clear understanding of the underlying structure of the situation. From this point of view, no good lawyer should ever forget that the farmer, no less than the rancher, is a potential planner of his activities. Indeed, assuming zero transaction costs, there were countless things the farmer might have done before the event to avoid the possible harm. He could have built an electric fence, say, to repel the cows abandoned by the lightning-struck cowboy. It is this failure to install the fence, no less than the rancher's refusal to hire an extra cowboy, that

6. The intuitive appeal, and the ultimate limits, of the reactive approach to causation can be appreciated by a study of R. Epstein, A Theory of Strict Liability: Toward a Reformulation of Tort Law (1980); Borgo, *Causal Paradigms in Tort Law*, 8 J. Leg. Stud. 419 (1979); Posner, *Epstein's Tort Theory: A Critique*, 8 J. Leg. Stud. 457 (1979); Epstein, *Causation and Corrective Justice: A Reply to Two Critics*, 8 J. Leg. Stud. 477 (1979).

the Coasean model identifies as a critical fact worthy of legal attention. Simply because this critical fact is less obvious from a superficial account of the cow-chomping incident, it should not be removed from the list of factors that helped to cause the harm. Instead of sifting the facts in search of *the* cause of the trouble, the lawyer-economist urges a conception of causation that recognizes how a multiplicity of factors, operating over a lengthy period of time, contribute to our legal discontents.[7]

But it is one thing to describe the way in which the assumption of zero transaction costs destabilizes the reactive lawyer's fact-finding enterprise, quite another to grasp how this single assumption could accomplish such a significant transformation. The answer may become clearer if we look upon lawyers as if they were storytellers, and "statements of the facts" as their effort to tell convincing stories. Now every good storyteller knows that the point at which the narrative begins will crucially shape the nature of the story line.[8] Events occurring before the story starts will inevitably be treated in a fragmentary way, as flashbacks justified only so far as they enlighten the course of unfolding events. In contrast, a credible storyteller must be more respectful of events occurring once the story has begun. After the "beginning," the tale must have a stronger narrative structure, linking events together in a compelling way until the story reaches its "end."

7. The most illuminating expression of this view by a lawyer-economist is to be found in Calabresi, *Concerning Cause and the Law of Torts: An Essay for Harry Kalven Jr.*, 43 U. CHI. L. REV. 69 (1975).

8. I am referring here to yarns of the Zane Grey type. Although the modernist novel has made us familiar with stories told in ways that fracture the traditional narrative's temporal and spatial structure, I shall not here consider the reasons why the law typically demands more traditional storytelling from its practitioners.

It is precisely here—on this critical narrative matter of beginnings and endings—that the assumption of zero transaction costs does its work. Rather than beginning with the moment at which the actors get into some form of obvious trouble, Coasean assumptions force the lawyer to start his story at a much earlier point in time: when the parties might have reorganized their activities in a way that could have avoided the trouble entirely. From this *ex ante* perspective, the harmful actions arising at a later time may only be symptoms of an earlier failure by rancher and farmer to organize their activities in the best possible way. In contrast, the reactive drama begins with the Coasean finale, the moment at which the cows start munching. While, on occasion, the reactive storyteller may feel obliged to flash back to some earlier moment to enlighten the parties' present struggle, the narrative focuses upon the trouble itself. Within this narrative framework, the rancher's failure to hire a second cowboy, or the farmer's failure to electrify his fence, are but two of the countless nonevents whose lengthy elaboration threatens to destroy the integrity of the tale of deviance and destruction that so urgently needs telling.

To summarize this first, and most critical, difference, I will borrow some useful terminology from Mark Kelman[9]

9. Kelman, *Interpretive Construction in the Substantive Criminal Law*, STAN. L. REV. 591, 593–594 (1981). As should be apparent, I also share Kelman's larger goal of explicating the interpretive frameworks prevailing in the contemporary American legal culture. Putting all questions of detail to one side, Kelman and I differ principally in the use to which we hope to put our project in legal consciousness-raising. The only question Kelman seriously entertains is whether his interpretive project is in the service of a neo-Marxist search for the subtle ways in which American law stabilizes class domination or a neo-Realist effort to demonstrate the pervasive importance of "inexplicably unpatterned mediators of experience, the inevitable nonrational filters we need to be

and say that the reactive lawyer employs a *narrow temporal frame* in stating his facts, focusing upon the culpability of the individual actions that constitute the obvious disturbance of the peace. In contrast, the Coasean insists upon a *broad temporal frame,* beginning at the moment foresighted men and women might possibly have reorganized their activities to avoid the trouble. The obvious problem itself serves as a symptom of a potentially larger problem of social disorganization.

Now this is just the transformation that is demanded by our model of activist legal discourse.[10] As we have seen, the activist lawyer cannot simply assume the legitimacy of the ongoing structure of activities, but must somehow be in a position to assess the extent to which these practices—here they are farming and ranching—require self-conscious restructuring through the legal order. The Coa-

---

able to perceive or talk at all." *Id.* at 671. For me, however, there is a third lesson American lawyers may draw from a deeper understanding of the principles implicit in their interpretive practice. Once the question of temporal framing is brought to legal self-consciousness, perhaps lawyers will be able to reflect more deeply upon the ways in which they are constructing legal reality and gradually proceed to make better sense of the politico-legal world in which they find themselves. Rather than accepting Kelman's interpretation of temporal framing as evidence of our collective nonrationality, we should recall Immanuel Kant's suggestion that the human capacity to interpret events in temporal terms provides a key to the proper understanding of human *rationality.* See I. KANT, CRITIQUE OF PURE REASON 139–140, 144–147 (Kemp-Smith ed. 1963).

In raising this more constructive possibility, I do not deny the pervasive reality of nonrational and/or repressive elements in any existing legal regime. But that is not *all* there is to our (or any?) legal system. Instead, the legal culture maintains a certain relative autonomy from other power systems, giving American lawyers the freedom to use their limited autonomy in thoughtful, as well as mindless, ways. Is it not a task of scholarship to support the constructive use of law's limited autonomy?

10. See Chapter 3.

sean's insistence that the legal story begins not with the trouble, but with the way the parties might have reorganized their activities to avoid it, is precisely the point at which the activist lawyer would *want* to begin.

· 2 ·

It is true, of course, that the next stage in the activist legal story—Coase's famous theorem—has been taken by many to teach a very different lesson: it warns us of the danger of overestimating the power of law to reorganize activities. But it is a bad mistake to confuse the cautionary character of a single theorem with the activist implications of the Coasean insistence that all legal stories begin at a new narrative starting point. After all, only a fool would imagine the task of reorganizing activities was a simple one. The existence of cautionary tales is an indispensable part of activist legal knowledge. Only when we can identify occasions upon which efforts at reorganization are futile may we focus the law's attention upon those cases in which reorganization seems worthwhile. Moreover, as cautionary tales go, the Coase theorem is pretty weak stuff. The crux, once again, is the critical role that the absence of transaction costs plays in Coase's cautionary conclusion. It is hardly dispiriting for an activist to learn that the law would not affect the way in which perfectly foresighted ranchers and farmers organized their activities in a world of frictionless transactions. Everybody is perfectly aware that the real world is no Coaseland, and that the Coase parable can therefore serve only as a prologue that demands completion by a systematic study of the countless difficulties confronting flesh and blood Americans as they try to organize their social lives. Indeed, the full Coasean statement of the facts is almost guaranteed to reveal a *rationality gap*—a complex set of real world structures that makes it impossible for actors to realize the hyperrational potential revealed by the Coasean prologue.

· 3 ·

Only at this point do the narrative accounts produced by different lawyer-economists begin to diverge. Though all are aware of the rationality gap, they disagree about the extent to which a "statement of the facts" loses legal credibility by failing to fill the gap with masses of thick description. Simplifiers treat the Coasean narrative as more-than-half-the-story. While they recognize the theoretical possibility of market failure, they always seem surprised when they encounter one in the real world, and they try their best to convince themselves that the rationality gap may be filled by some very interstitial form of judicial intervention. Complexifiers, in contrast, treat the Coase theorem as a prologue to a three-part drama: act one, the elaboration of an intricate web of market imperfections; act two, the emphatic denial of the possibility of a perfect solution; act three, the complex description of the ways in which actors, constrained by heavy transaction costs and bounded rationality, are likely to respond to an array of second-best legal interventions.

Now, so far as each particular lawyer is concerned, the choice between simplicity and complexity will be resolved by a host of personal, political, and even aesthetic motivations.[11] Rather than indulging in curbstone psychoanaly-

11. Yielding an analytic product that ranges from the crude simplifications typical of textbooks like R. POSNER, ECONOMIC ANALYSIS OF LAW (2d ed. 1977), to the complexities characteristic of monographs auth-

sis, however, I am more interested in the long-term movement of professional culture. Here there is reason to anticipate a generational drift toward increasingly complex narrative. For the very success of the simplifiers in gaining attention for their distinctive language of power is the thing that will prove their ultimate undoing. While the elegance and counterintuitive character of the Coase theorem is a heady brew indeed for those accustomed to a Realist diet of particularistic fact and intuitionist value, the shock effect achieved by the simplifier only serves to begin a larger process of cultural assimilation. The deeper and broader the Coasean penetration into legal conversation, the less the theorem will seem a disturbing novelty, the more it will seem a familiar tool of factual analysis.

And in the law at least, familiarity breeds the very reverse of contempt. As soon as lawyers are convinced that arguing about transaction costs may win cases, they can be relied upon to complexify the new conceptual apparatus in any way that will suit their client's interest. Over time, it will become increasingly clear that the varieties of transactional failure are almost infinite and that the profession must develop an elaborate set of categories if it

---

ored by G. CALABRESI, THE COSTS OF ACCIDENTS (1970), and G. CALABRESI & P. BOBBITT, TRAGIC CHOICES (1978). It should be noted that Coase's seminal article itself was delicately poised between simplicity and complexity: while the essay begins with its pathbreaking speculations about economic and legal life in a world without transaction cost, it concludes with a strong affirmation of the importance of transactional imperfection in serious law and economics. Compare Coase, *supra* note 1, at 2–8, with pp. 15–19 from the same article. At about the time Coase was writing his essay, Calabresi was reaching similar conclusions in work proceeding independently of Coasean influence. See his *Some Thoughts on Risk Distribution and the Law of Torts*, 70 YALE L. J. 499 (1961), and his *Decision for Accidents: An Approach to Nonfault Allocation of Costs*, 78 HARV. L. REV. 713 (1965).

hopes to complete the Coasean prologue in a way that is equal to the wide range of transactional structures revealed by the stream of cases. The predictable result is that the initial parable of the rancher and the farmer will begin to seem a rather easy case of an externality—in which only "imperfect information" and the costs of negotiating a full set of "contingency contracts" impede the parties' capacity to reorganize their activities. Other cases will reveal a deeper set of structural impediments. When held up to the light of the Coasean model, our real world will come to seem a place full of pervasive transactional problems with many names: "free ride," "moral hazard," "bounded rationality," "nonconvex demand and supply curves," "imperfections in capital markets," and so forth, each requiring systematic attention in the analysis of one or another market failure.[12]

This new form of factual analysis, moreover, provides a powerful impetus for legal generalizations of a kind quite alien to our Realist predecessors. As the complexifying Coasean states his version of the facts in more and more cases, it becomes ever clearer that different branches of the law treat similar market failures in very different ways. "Nuisance," "products liability," and "fault," for example, now seem different common law labels for handling a complex set of interrelated problems organized by the existence of a complex variety of externalities and related market failures. Since lawyers are taught that like cases should be treated alike, this perception of factual

12. While lawyers can take advantage of an already enormous, and rapidly expanding, technical literature in economics on all these subjects, the work that will have the largest impact will combine technical mastery over the anatomy of transactional failure with a genuine appreciation of legal and institutional complexity. For a seminal contribution of this kind, see O. WILLIAMSON, MARKETS AND HIERARCHIES (1975).

similarity generates a cognitive drive for a new synthesis. Hasn't the time come to think the externality question through in a systematic way, reconstructing the law to deal responsively with the facts that the new analysis reveals to view?[13]

This question applies with even greater force to the disordered heap of statutory law that dominates today's legal landscape. While the previous generation could see little beyond a mass of particular statutory formulae disguising enormous administrative discretion, Coasean lawyers are quick to find that their understanding of market failure permits them a new view of the statutory terrain. Vast forests of detail—previously consigned to the wilderness of environmental law or health and safety legislation or oil and gas law or securities regulation—can be reduced to cognitively manageable terms as soon as they are seen as efforts to come to grips with a series of interrelated market failures. This perception, moreover, makes it possible for legal specialists to increase their range of reference as they debate the proper way of responding to problems arising under their particular statutory regime. While a layman might think that there is almost nothing in common between, say, the problems raised by securities fraud and those raised by air pollution, a common externality analysis makes it possible for lawyers in one field to learn from the regulatory experience in the other.[14] The ground is being prepared for a professionally disciplined effort to

13. For a particularly influential Constructive answer to this question, see Calabresi & Melamed, *One View of the Cathedral: Property Rules, Liability Rules and Inalienability*, 85 HARV. L. REV. 1089 (1972).

14. Not that the problems are identical, of course, but that only makes the comparative market failure/legal response analysis only more interesting.

compare and assess a broad range of responses to market failure—whether they be primarily shaped by judges, bureaucrats, or legislators—in terms of a common legal language.[15]

## Extending the Paradigm

The Coasean transformation of torts is not only important in itself; it is also paradigmatic[16] of a larger effort by lawyers to reconstruct their understanding of "the facts" throughout the length and breadth of the legal culture. While this essay cannot hope to establish such a sweeping claim, two brief extensions of the analysis may at least serve to render the hypothesis plausible.[17]

15.  In this regard, Judge Stephen Breyer's book REGULATION AND ITS REFORM (1982) marks a breakthrough, not so much in the novelty of its conceptual apparatus, but in its systematic and balanced application of the new learning to a host of legal problems characteristic of an activist state. Rather than a pathbreaking article (Coase), or a brilliant monograph (Calabresi), or a student textbook (Posner), Judge Breyer has produced a lawbook that speaks in a persuasive way to lawyers grappling with the practical problems of activist legislation, administration, and (to a lesser extent) adjudication. Even more important in this respect is the eight-volume treatise by P. AREEDA & D. TURNER, ANTITRUST LAW: AN ANALYSIS OF ANTITRUST PRINCIPLES AND THEIR APPLICATION (vols. 1, 2, 3, 1978; vols. 4, 5, 1980; vols. 6, 7, forthcoming; vol. 8, 1982). It marks the first time that practitioners of the new learning have ever aspired to the legal authority that is uniquely associated with the treatise form.

16.  This is not the place to enter into the definitional wars surrounding Thomas Kuhn's use of the idea of a paradigm in his seminal work, *The Structure of Scientific Revolutions* (2d. ed. 1970). It would be disingenuous, however, to deny that Kuhn's work has been a source of inspiration for the present essay.

17.  A recent Symposium, published after work on this book was completed, contains a good deal of material that is relevant to an assessment of my hypothesis. See generally, Symposium, *The Place of Economics in Legal Education*, 33 J. LEG. EDUC. 183 (1983).

· *1* ·

The first extension follows the Coasean reformulation from its origin in torts to neighboring legal domains. To see the potential here, simply use classical legal language to describe the way in which the Coasean manages the movement from a narrow to a broad temporal framing of the standard torts dispute. By beginning each torts dispute from an earlier point in time, Coase invites us, as it were, to look upon all torts problems as if they began as problems of contract—in which farsighted farmers and ranchers might bargain their way to a well-defined solution. If this emphasis on contract, however, permits a new perspective on torts, might it not also permit a new perspective on contracts?

The answer is yes, and yet there are paradoxes aplenty in the rebirth of contract heralded by Constructive lawyers. At the same time they insist upon the continuing importance of voluntary bargaining, Constructive lawyers hope to make good upon the Realists' insight into the limits of contract. The new typology of transaction failure permits a systematic examination of the inadequacies of contract with a rigor unknown in the Realist tradition. Not only do the very same transactional difficulties afflicting tort law—imperfect information, externality, and so forth—also pervade contractual settings. There is also a host of new difficulties that are even more salient in contract than they were in torts: "moral hazard," "monitoring costs," "first mover advantages," and the like.[18]

18. See, e.g., Goetz & Scott, *Principles of Relational Contracts*, 67 Va. L. Rev. 1089 (1981); Schwartz & Wilde, *Intervening in Markets on the Basis of Imperfect Information: A Legal and Economic Analysis*, 127 U. Pa. L. Rev. 630 (1979); Williamson, *The Governance of Contractual Relations*, 22 J. Law & Econ. 233 (1979).

This recognition serves, in turn, as a second source of Constructive energy for new kinds of legal generalization. No longer is the treatment of contract focused exclusively upon the classic excuses and justifications of interest to the reactive lawyer—mistake, impossibility, and so forth.[19] Precisely because contract is a systematically defective tool for coordination, there is a perceived need to assess the extent to which other legal forms can permit people to transcend the frictions of the contractual setting. Moreover, each of these forms—from the old law of principal and agent through the modern forms of partnership and corporation through the varieties of government ownership and regulation—is found, soon enough, to solve the transactional problems of contract only at the cost of generating new kinds of transactional difficulties of its own. Once again, the stage is being set for a complex, yet broad-based analysis of the way in which activist law, by controlling the legal forms provided to the parties, can shape the way they use their legal freedom to plan their activities.[20]

Beyond its more particular conclusions, the emphasis upon contractual failure reinforces the sense that the specific troubles brought to the attention of courts, agencies, and legislatures may well be only the symptoms of some deeper organizational failure. As in torts, so in contracts, Constructive analysis forces the legal conversation to

19.  Although these classical issues will, predictably, be subjected to reanalysis, see, e.g., the essays collected by A. KRONMAN & R. POSNER, THE ECONOMICS OF CONTRACT LAW (1979).

20.  In addition to Williamson's work cited *supra* notes 12 and 18, the seminal contribution of Jensen & Meckling, *Theory of the Firm: Managerial Behavior, Agency Costs and Ownership Structure*, 3 J. FIN. ECON. 305 (1976), has prompted a renewed appreciation of the roots of corporate structure in contractual failure—a lesson that Coase taught long ago in *The Nature of the Firm*, 4 ECONOMICA 386 (1937).

begin at a new point—starting the story with the possibility that the law might reconstruct organizational forms in ways that allow citizens to ameliorate, if not eliminate, the conflicts that appear so intractable on the surface of everyday life.

· 2 ·

It is odd, perhaps, to think of the second extension of Coasean analysis as an extension at all. Chronologically at least, the lawyer-economist's description of reality first achieved professional recognition not in the fields of torts and contracts but in public law areas such as antitrust and regulated industries.[21] Indeed, the existence of these conversational beachheads helps explain the Coaseans' more recent successes in penetrating the legal culture. However disturbing Realistic lawyers may find talk of externality or contract failure, they cannot deny that the relevance of similar sounding stuff is an established professional fact across the dim boundary that separates private from public law in an activist state.[22] Yet, despite its priority in time and its continuing legal importance, I do not think it wrong to subordinate the old "law and economics" to the

21. See, e.g., C. KAYSEN & D. TURNER, ANTI-TRUST POLICY: AN ECO-NOMIC AND LEGAL ANALYSIS (1959); L. SCHWARTZ, FREE ENTERPRISE AND ECONOMIC ORGANIZATION (1952). Indeed, Coase himself can be understood to have achieved his breakthrough in tort law by generalizing the transactional approach to questions of industrial organization he had developed earlier. See his *The Nature of the Firm, supra* note 20; *The Federal Communications Commission*, 2 J. LAW & ECON. 1 (1959). Given the historical depth of the lawyer-economist's treatment of the industrial organization question, it is hardly surprising that the new learning has first expressed itself in the form of an authoritative treatise in this area, P. AREEDA & D. TURNER, ANTITRUST LAW, *supra* note 15.

22. See Chapter 3.

new in this sketch of the present legal situation. For, so long as the use of "law and economics" was restricted to a small number of specialities, the distinctive character of the antitrust lawyers' construction of reality could be plausibly viewed as a cultural phenomenon of purely local legal significance—on a par, say, with the use and abuse of psychoanalytic discourse by the criminal lawyer when dealing with the insanity defense. It is only with the new "law and economics" that the movement becomes a genuine challenge to Realist orthodoxy. For it then becomes plain that Realism is being challenged not only here-and-there but almost everywhere by lawyers drawing from a common fund of Constructive ideas. The cultural whole is becoming larger than the sum of its parts. When the old "law and economics" is added to the new, the result does not add up to two specialist legal discourses but a general legal discourse.

Indeed, this fact is signaled by the way in which the old "law and economics" takes on more general legal meaning for lawyers in legal fields who were sublimely indifferent to it in the past. No longer isolated specialties, "antitrust" and "regulation" mark conversational areas in which the structural descriptions increasingly familiar in torts and contracts are generalized yet further: from this-or-that struggle between rancher and farmer, this-or-that response to contractual failure, to the way entire sectors of the economy (fail to) relate to one another.[23] As in the more microscopic forms of structural analysis, legal con-

23. Not that economic efficiency is necessarily all there is to antitrust. Even those—and I am one of them—who resist the Chicago reduction of antitrust policy to economic efficiency, in the manner of Bork's The Antitrust Paradox: A Policy at War with Itself (1978), would hardly deny that the economist's "statement of the facts" is an essential preliminary to the mature legal discussion of the political and economic values at stake in the law of industrial organization.

versation begins here with an imaginary prologue about life in a frictionless world inhabited by hyperrational actors capable of understanding all the implications of their organizational activities. Once again, however, the analysis of the frictionless world of perfect competition can only serve as a prologue for real-world analysis, in which one gains an understanding of the way firms exploit underlying production possibilities and a host of transactional barriers to gain competitive advantages over potential rivals. As always, some lawyer-economists—the Chicagoans—tend to become impatient at this point in the story. Just as they would like lawyers to talk torts as if they lived in a world very close to Coase's never-never land, so too they are happiest when talking about antitrust in a world that seriously departs from perfect competition only rarely and in well-understood ways. But there is nothing that forces the rest of us to mistake the prologue for the play.

## Enriching the Paradigm

We find ourselves, then, in the midst of a very rare event in the life of the law: the rise to professional maturity of a new construction of the facts. This is suggested not only by the breadth of legal application of the Coasean construction, but also by the increasing complexity with which the Coasean narrative can be adapted to take a multitude of real-world "imperfections" into account. How, then, to make the most of our maturity?

· *1* ·

Beginning on the technical level, it is not too early to call for the next advance in activist fact-finding sophistication.

It is one thing, say, to recognize that the Clean Air Act can be viewed as a response to a complex set of externalities or that ERISA, the federal statute regulating private pensions, may be viewed as a complex response to the problems of contractual failure. It is quite another thing to make the concrete factual findings necessary to frame a professional discussion of the extent to which the Air Act or ERISA can, through proper bureaucractic and judicial interpretation as well as legislative revision, be made into *appropriate* legal responses to the structural problems that have been identified. To take this step, we cannot content ourselves with a graphic description of Smokestack No. 9's belching black discharges or a story about the way loyal Mary Jones was deprived of her pension by the sudden failure of Bankrupt Inc. While such anecdotes may catalyze concern, we must set them in a larger context, systematically describing the way a mass of industrial emissions moves from air-shed to air-shed to cause pollution of concern to the Clean Air Act, or the way people move from job to job on their path to an impoverished retirement of conern to ERISA.

To appraise these facts competently, we will have to abandon one of the most cherished beliefs handed down to us by our Realist predecessors. As we have seen, the last legal generation made opposition to something they called "formalism" or "arid conceptualism" a defining feature of their intellectual accommodation to the New Deal. Yet it is precisely such epithets that stand in the way of a serious professional effort to face up to the lawyer's fact-finding responsibilities in an activist state. Whatever may have been true during an earlier time, formalism can no longer be taken to imply an attitude of blind indifference to the facts of social life. Instead, it is continuing hostility to formalism that will condemn lawyers to fact-finding impotence in the modern era. Quite simply, we are already in the midst of a revolution in information processing that permits, for the first time in history, a disciplined empirical analysis of the structural facts of central importance to activist legal decision. Increasingly, the call for an appropriate "statement of the facts" will generate mountains of computer printout detailing a proliferating number of scenarios of obvious relevance to responsible activist decisionmaking. Until such time as lawyers understand the *formal* economic, political, and sociological presuppositions of particular computer analyses, they can play only three roles in the fact-finding process. Most obviously, they may play the obscurantist and deny that the computer printout is worth the paper it is written on; or they may worship blindly before the shiny new shrine of the American Enlightenment and believe everything the computer tells them (so long as it is not patently absurd); or they may play the moralizer and make sure that the manipulators of the black box are not obviously corrupt or biased. And of course, they may combine all three poses in the endless permutations known to every student of modern administrative law.

The only thing they will not be able to do is to engage in a meaningful dialogue with the model builders concerning the basic assumptions that guided them in their construction of the social reality with which the law will have to deal. Yet it is *only* through this dialogue that lawyers can help unearth a host of controversial legal questions that are raised in every effort to state the structural facts. While a conversation between lawyers and modelers can misfire even under the best of institutional conditions, administrative law cannot even begin to take the institutional problems seriously when lawyers are professionally incapable of carrying on their side of the dialogue. Until the profession achieves minimal computer competence, the legal pursuit of activist values will increasingly proceed on the basis of a "statement of the facts" that begs all sorts of fundamental legal questions.[24]

Not that every competent lawyer must be put into a position to manipulate the latest computer software package on his own. The key here, as elsewhere, is to permit the individual to ask the right questions, questions that arise time after time in appraising the computer construction of legal reality. My own experience teaching such matters[25] suggests, moreover, that a good deal could be achieved along these lines in a relatively short period of time—certainly no more time than the average law student characteristically devotes to the mysteries of trial practice and the law of evidence.[26] What is lacking at present, however, is a general recognition of the pressing legal importance of questioning computers with the same seriousness that we already invest in cross-examining eye witnesses to the disturbing events that catalyze the concern of reactive lawyers. It is, in short, past time to redeem Holmes's century-old prediction that the future of the law belongs to the master of statistics, no less than economics.[27] Indeed, the fact that we still allow law students to graduate without the slightest understanding of statistical reasoning and formal modeling is nothing short of a scandalous

24. This theme will be elaborated further in Chapter 6.

25. Of the kind addressed in B. ACKERMAN, S. ROSE-ACKERMAN, J. SAWYER, & D. HENDERSON, THE UNCERTAIN SEARCH FOR ENVIRONMENTAL QUALITY (1974), and B. ACKERMAN & W. HASSLER, CLEAN COAL/DIRTY AIR (1981).

26. Moreover, entering students can be expected to come to law school with an increasingly sophisticated store of computer lore, thereby making the pedagogic task more manageable over time.

27. Holmes, *The Path of the Law*, 10 HARV L. REV. 457, 461 (1897).

dereliction of our professional responsibilities.[28] If we continue down this misguided path, we will in the end break a fundamental promise made by the New Deal: that American lawyers can indeed help keep the law responsive to the changing facts of social life in a way that promotes the activist concerns of their fellow Americans.

There is, of course, a danger here. The Constructive lawyer of the future may become a computer addict who is obtuse to any fact he cannot model and quantify. The best cure for such a disease, however, is some thoughtful professional training in the uses and abuses of computer modeling in the activist legal process. For the next generation, moreover, the more serious legal pathologies will arise from acute computer anemia, rather than computer addiction. In particular, a profession of statistical innocents will tend unduly to fixate upon the just-so stories the simplifying Chicagoan will be happy to tell about life in Coaseland, rather than push onward to the concrete investigation of the transactional failures that arise in the real world. For the Chicago tales about never-never land can be mastered by a lawyer who believes that "multiple regression" is the name of some arcane Freudian affliction. In contrast, a professionally sophisticated activist lawyer must learn to distinguish mediocre but useable regression analysis from truly awful computer garbage.

28. Indeed, insofar as the computer is entering legal education, it is as an instructional gimmick, allowing the student a new form of interactive instruction that may usefully complement more traditional forms of pedagogy. See F. Michelman and the Harvard Law School Committee on Educational Planning and Development, Computer Aided Instruction (1982) (unpublished report, tentative final draft). While I have no doubt that programmed learning ought to occupy an important place in legal education, this is *not* the kind of instruction I am advocating here. Rather than programming computers to teach law to lawyers, I am interested in educating lawyers to keep computers under legal control.

If we are to move beyond Chicago simplicities, the cure must be more computer modeling, rather than less; a deeper appreciation of the complexities of market failure and probabilistic inference, rather than an uncritical attack on formalism in all its forms.[29] For it is only then that lawyers may focus, in a disciplined way, upon the empirical guesswork that is required if the activist state is to confront maturely the difficulties involved in ameliorating the rigors of the invisible hand. In short, the more lawyers can control their Realist impatience with the formal character of statistical analysis, the better they will discharge their fact-finding functions.

· 2 ·

The same is true when it comes to the next generation's effort to move beyond the more fundamental limitations of the Coasean construction of reality. I very much hope, for example, that the Coasean description of market phenomena will encourage lawyerly dissatisfaction with the platitudes we continue to tolerate in the professional discussion of political and bureaucratic processes. A move beyond banality, however, will require us to confront the impressive work of the past generation of political economists, despite the fact that some of this work requires some simple formal logic for its ready comprehension.[30]

29. While critical theorists have been emphatic in their condemnation of formalism—see, e.g., Kennedy, *Legal Formality, supra* chap. 2, note 11, at 377–391, and Kennedy, *Form and Substance, supra* chap. 2, note 9—they have not yet, so far as I know, specifically focused upon the use of the computer in activist fact-finding. Is it too late to hope that a more discriminating critical attitude toward formalism may yet emerge?

30. In addition to the works cited in chap. 3, note 11, important writings include M. OLSON, THE LOGIC OF COLLECTIVE ACTION (1971); A.

Nevertheless, a Constructivist theory that focuses upon the varieties of market failure without paying equal attention to the reality of political and bureaucratic failure is transparently inadequate.

It is no less obvious that the present-day Coasean has not even begun to consider how the law shapes social perception and evaluation through a complex process of education and indoctrination.[31] Although this is a very great failing, it simply serves to mark Coaseanism, despite its triumph in redefining the legal time frame and refocusing attention upon the reorganization of activities, as a very primitive form of Constructive thought. It is a strength, rather than a weakness, of the present moment that this failure is so plain to view. Collective dissatisfaction serves as the best prod for deeper Construction in the years ahead.

HIRSCHMAN, EXIT, VOICE, AND LOYALTY (1970); D. BLACK, THE THEORY OF COMMITTEES AND ELECTIONS (1958); A. DOWNS, AN ECONOMIC THEORY OF DEMOCRACY (1957); K. ARROW, SOCIAL CHOICE AND INDIVIDUAL VALUES (1951).

31. I wish I could report a breakthrough here, but at present we remain very much at the pronunciamento stage. For a usefully skeptical review of the sociological literature, see Hyde, *The Concept of Legitimation in the Sociology of Law*, 1983 WISC. L. REV. 379; for an illuminating effort to reinvigorate Weberian insights, see A. KRONMAN, MAX WEBER (1983); for my own choices in contemporary cultural anthropology and sociology, see Ackerman, *Four Questions*, *supra* chap. 3, note 1, at 372 and notes 41–44.

# · 5 ·
# Constructing Legal Values

---

THE CONSTRUCTIVE EFFORT to "state the facts" does more than impose new cognitive demands upon lawyers who wish to perform credibly in the modern age. It also places great pressure on the legal culture to develop a form of value analysis equal to its developing powers of Constructive description. On the one hand, the focus on structural facts undercuts the foundations of the Realist's intuitionistic approach to value articulation. On the other, it prepares the way for a new kind of legal dialogue that seeks to explicate the complex character of the struggle for social justice in a liberal activist state.

## Beyond Realism

Quite simply, Constructivist description of complex market processes puts into question the Realist's prized possession—the crafty "situation sense" that allows him to respond to the facts of a particular case by modifying the working rules of the legal tradition in the light of half-formed intuitions about the values legitimized by the New Deal and its successors. For it suddenly comes to seem that the savvy Realist has been nourishing his moral intuitions with the wrong kinds of facts. Rather than telling himself anecdotes about how one or another actor provoked some trouble that ended up in litigation, he should have begun the legal story much earlier, starting from the point at which market imperfections hampered the participants' efforts to reorganize their activities in light of existing and proposed legal rules. From this new narrative starting point, the Realist's heroic efforts at particularistic intuition seem more naïve than realistic.

Take one example: the effort by common law courts to adapt the traditional law of landlord–tenant relations to suit activist notions of distributive justice. Concerned about the inequality of bargaining power between slum landlords and tenants, activist courts throughout the country have imposed a warranty of habitability upon leases in an effort to improve the quality of housing available to impoverished slum tenants. The most important thing to ask about these cases is not whether they are right or wrong, but how mature and intelligent judges could fail, in framing their decisions, to make a serious effort to inform themselves about the structure of the rental market they confront. For it is only on the basis of such an inquiry that they could even make an intelligent guess as to whether the warranty does indeed benefit most poor tenants. Not that the "conservative" judges opposing this "liberal" trend do any better. While some may raise vague doubts as to the consequences of it all, they are no more interested in gathering and assessing the hard empirical evidence than their liberal antagonists. The hard truth seems to be that the present judicial generation possesses neither the professional training nor the inclination to make even the crudest guesses about the distributive consequences of their rulings. Worse yet, they do not even know what they are missing, having made their Realistic peace with the New Deal by thinking small, instead of placing their particular conflict within a larger framework of structural description.

However popular this strategy may be with today's judiciary,[1] it hardly assures the survival of their proud creation in an increasingly Constructive future. As the Coasean framework entrenches itself in the legal culture, it will no longer suffice to justify the warranty of habitability by telling one or another horror story about indecent accommodations. Rather than invoking *ex post* anecdotes, the decisive questions will be whether, *ex ante,* the warranty will benefit slum dwellers as a class; and if so, whether egalitarian redistribution is an affirmative value in our legal system; and if so, whether it is fairer to pursue these egalitarian objectives by reshaping common law forms like warranty, or by devising new public law forms like the negative income tax, or both. What is needed, in short, is not an extra heavy dose of particularistic intuition, but some sustained argument about the nature of activist justice and the modalities of its legal vindication. This need is already being recognized in the legal literature. Predictably, the Chicagoans have entered their denunciations of

1. For a snapshot of the complex judicial situation at present, see Browder, *The Taming of a Duty—The Tort Liability of Landlords,* 81 U. MICH. L. REV. 99 (1982).

the inefficiencies of the warranty.[2] More significantly, the friends of the warranty have begun to recognize the inadequacy of the intuitionistic defense and the necessity of explicating the conditions under which the so-called private law may legitimately serve as a vehicle for egalitarian values.[3] The groundwork is being laid for a warranty law far more sensitive to the complexities of activist justice than the muddle bequeathed to us by the past generation.

Turning from Realistic courts to "expert" agencies, Constructivism will generate a similar disenchantment with the intuitionistic style of agency decisionmaking concealed by New Deal deference to "administrative discretion." Until the profession had stabilized a method of cogently describing the relevant structural facts, it was in no position to question too closely the bureaucrats' use of their power. However mythic the claim of expertise in one or another case, lawyers had little choice but to indulge the myth so long as they themselves could not profess a disciplined understanding of the structural facts in dis-

2. R. POSNER, ECONOMIC ANALYSIS OF LAW, 356–358 (2d ed. 1977); Komesar, *Return to Slumville: A Critique of the Ackerman Analysis of Housing Code Enforcement and the Poor*, 82 YALE L. J. 1175 (1973).

3. Ackerman, *Regulating Slum Housing Markets on Behalf of the Poor: Of Housing Codes, Housing Subsidies and Income Redistribution Policy*, 80 YALE L. J. 1093 (1971); Abbott, *Housing Policy, Housing Codes and Tenant Remedies: An Integration*, 56 B. U. L. REV. 1 (1976); Markovits, *Distributive Impact, Allocative Efficiency, and Overall Desirability of Ideal Housing Codes: Some Theoretical Clarifications*, 89 HARV. L. REV. 1815 (1976); Kennedy, *Distributive and Paternalist Motives in Contract and Tort Law, With Special Reference to Compulsory Terms and Unequal Bargaining Power*, 41 MD. L. REV. 563 (1982). The debate has even generated some primitive statistical work on the issue, see Hirsch, Hirsch & Margolis, *Regression Analysis of the Effect of Habitability Laws upon Rent: An Empirical Observation on the Ackerman-Komesar Debate*, 63 CAL. L. REV. 1098 (1975); Hirsch, *Landlord-Tenant Relations Law*, in THE ECONOMIC APPROACH TO LAW 277 (Burrows & Veljanovski eds. 1981).

pute. For the scrutiny of mythic experts by legal know-
nothings would only further erode the central principle of
activist legitimacy—the notion that *somewhere* within the
state apparatus lies an institutional intelligence capable of
regulating, for the public good, the social structures
thrown up by the invisible hand. Given the absence of a
Constructive set of tools for describing structural facts, the
most lawyers could hope to do was to check the worst
abuses of discretion by complexifying administrative pro-
cedure.

Once the profession gains a semblance of cognitive control over the facts, however, it can afford to take a very different attitude toward administrative discretion. Rather
than an assault upon the activist state, legal review of the
substance of administrative regulation will begin to seem
appropriate preventive medicine for the ultimate activist
dis-ease: Is it not obvious that if we allow claims of expertise to rest on a heap of computer output, we do not merely
risk incompetence and corruption, but bureaucratic tyranny?

Increasingly, it will seem plausible for lawyers to try to
persuade agencies that they have misunderstood the
structure of the activities they regulate. When bureaucrats persist in ignoring the relevant market failures,
moreover, lawyers for affected interests can be expected to
appeal for corrective action. Now that they can describe
the structural facts, they will have every incentive to articulate legal principles that reveal the agency to be abusing
its discretion, and demand a hearing for their increasingly
refined complaints about the substance of administrative
policy. This does not imply, of course, that traditional
courts of appeal will monopolize the legal effort to articulate principles that can *incisively* guide agency rulemak-

ing. Instead, the perceived need to test administrative discretion in Constructive ways will generate a host of institutional experiments. Old institutions, like the National Academy of Sciences, will be given increasingly important review functions.[4] Acronymic entities, like RARG and GAO, will spring to life in corners of the Executive branch and in the Congress.[5]

In self-defense, agencies will not only tend to assimilate the legally prevailing forms of structural description into their own fact-finding efforts. They will also try to justify themselves in the light of principles emerging from the ongoing process of Constructive review—whether they are principles of cost-benefit analysis or distributive justice (or both). And when particular regulatory initiatives do not seem readily rationalizeable within the new legal rhetoric, even agency bureaucrats will sense that their programs are anomalies ripe for law reform. Some agencies will, of course, respond to their anomalous status by building the powerful political and economic alliances necessary to survive in a hostile cultural environment. I am not

4. See, e.g., the complex pattern of interaction between the National Academy of Sciences, the EPA, Congress, and the courts revealed in *International Harvester* v. *Ruckelshaus*, 478 Fed. 615 (D.C. Cir. 1973) (Leventhal, J.).

5. The role of the Carter administration's RARG—the Regulatory Analysis Review Group—is discussed in B. ACKERMAN & W. HASSLER. CLEAN COAL/DIRTY AIR, chap. 6 (1981); the further evolution of executive branch oversight during the Reagan administration is sketched in Viscusi, *Presidential Oversight: Controlling the Regulators*, 2 J. POL. ANAL. & MAN. 157 (1983). The role of the General Accounting Office is discussed in Litke & O'Connor, *The Changing Role and Influence of the GAO on Regulation*, 106 PUB. UTIL. 25 (1980); J. Singer, *When the Evaluators Are Evaluated, the GAO Often Gets Low Marks*, 11 NAT. J. 1889 (1979). For a thoughtful assessment of the weaknesses of present oversight institutions, see R. LITAN & W. NORDHAUS, REFORMING FEDERAL REGULATION 59–99 (1983).

concerned here, however, with the fate of any particular regulatory regime. My point is to emphasize the dynamic by which a legally stabilized form of structural description undercuts the rhetorical force of appeals to administrative discretion. Rather than a Realistic description of an intractable reality, "discretion" will come to seem the last resort of an agency that has lost touch with the facts of social life.

## The Search for Legal Value

It is one thing to destabilize Realistic intuitionism in private and public law; it is quite another to fashion a form of legal discourse that might plausibly take its place. Indeed, the very success in destabilizing intuitionistic adjudication and bureaucratic discretion makes the need for Constructive value-talk more urgent. Once we have resolved to transcend our New Deal muddle, how are we to define the occasions when the law must self-consciously intervene to aid in the creation of a more humane and just society? How do we tell a market failure from a market success? What *are* the legal values endangered by the uncontrolled operation of the invisible hand?

It will not do to respond to these questions by peremptorily ruling them off the profession's conversational agenda. While a legal system governed by reactive political premises may plausibly consign such issues to a far-off conversational domain inhabited by philosophers or politicians, such a dramatic truncation of professional discourse would make it impossible for American lawyers to make sense of their activist legal world.[6] Fifty years after the

6. See Chapter 3.

New Deal, too many lawyers are all too familiar with the sight of a desk heaped high with bureaucratic edicts, judicial opinions, and legislative commands. If they are to shape this raw material into persuasive arguments, they can hardly avoid reflecting upon the more general activist values that putatively justify all this legal activity.

Yet, though the prevailing rationales for government intervention will become a principal subject for lawyerly conversation, the need for *some* kind of professional discipline will remain undiminished. In a democratic activist state, it is up to the People, and not their lawyers, to decide upon the activist principles that will inform the legal system.[7] If lawyers do not like the principles, $P$, that the People have chosen, they can try to persuade the People to change their mind. In the meantime, they have a democratic obligation to use $P$ in legal argument, rather than the not-$P$ they favor in politics. How, then, do we identify those activist principles that have already been endorsed by the People and distinguish them from the not-$P$'s that are still struggling for recognition in the agon of democratic politics?

It would be nice, I suppose, if the People's representatives were good enough to state their activist principles clearly and incisively on the surface of their legislation. In the half-century since the New Deal, however, American lawyers have begun to reconcile themselves to the reality of a very different legal world, one full of dim light and half shadow.

Not that our legal picture is entirely gray on gray. Certain things *are* so plain as to be beyond serious argument. Thus, it is no longer plausible to assert that American law

7. See Chapter 3.

is governed by strict adherence to Lockean principles of laissez-faire government; it is equally silly to suppose that the New Deal ushered in an era of Marxist collectivism. While right- and left-wing excursions into doctrinal analysis may well contain valuable insights, they will inevitably oversimplify our present legal situation, whose distinctive complexity is generated by the New Deal's effort to depart from Lockean laissez faire *without* taking the path to Marxist collectivism. The challenge, in short, is to make sense of the distinctive topography of a legal system that aims to occupy the high middle ground disdained by the followers of Locke and Marx alike. How, then, do we elaborate the aims of a legal system that is activist without being authoritarian, liberal without being libertarian?

## The Poverty of Welfare Economics

It is here, once again, that the lawyer-economist is all too eager to offer assistance to the puzzled Constructivist. If economics permits a disciplined way of talking about the facts of market life, will it not also answer the normative questions it allows us to raise in a newly disciplined fashioned?

The slightest degree of historical perspective should caution against an overly eager yes. Economics, after all, has suffered its own ordeals during the last half-century. Most important for our purposes is its extraordinary success in purging itself of explicit and elaborate reflection on its relation to the broader problems of political philosophy.[8]

8. A philosophically sophisticated history of intellectual developments in Anglo-American economics over the past half-century has yet

Perhaps this absolute divorce from philosophy was the price economists had to pay for their century-long marriage to English utilitarianism. The only way to free the profession from its former love was to assure it that the entire question utilitarianism sought to answer was utterly meaningless. Perhaps, as many economists themselves believe, good positive economics requires the profession to draw a hard positivist line against the infection of factual findings by subjective value judgments. In any event, a pervasive suspicion of elaborate value-talk is now a deeply rooted professional prejudice amongst economists—that will take a long time to undo, if undoing there is to be.[9] In the meantime, however, the profession's strong positivist prejudices must be taken into account by any lawyer who wants to master economics for law's purposes, rather than the other way around.

Before following the Chicagoan on a quick raid across the disciplinary frontier in quest of "economic efficiency,"

to be written. See the clever review of the literature by McCloskey, *The Rhetoric of Economics*, 21 J. Econ. Lit. 481 (1983). For the canonical decree establishing an absolute divorce between economics and philosophy, see L. Robbins, On the Nature and Significance of Economic Science chap. 6 (1932), whose arguments betray a naïve self-confidence in the logical positivism then so important in English philosophy. The frequency with which Robbins is still parroted a half-century later provides the best index of the extent to which professional economists have insulated themselves from the main currents of contemporary philosophy.

9. At the moment, the most important philosophical voice within economics is surely Amartya Sen's. See, e.g., his *Utilitarianism and Welfarism*, 76 J. Phil. 463 (1979); *Rational Fools: A Critique of the Behavioral Foundations of Economic Theory*, 6 Phil. & Pub. Aff. 317 (1977). Unfortuantely, Sen's philosophical interests, like those of Kenneth Arrow in the preceding generation, may turn out to be so exceptional that they merely confirm the profession's pronounced positivistic prejudices.

Constructive lawyers must recognize that the discipline of welfare economics was not formulated with their interpretive needs in mind. To put it mildly, Hicks, Kaldor, Scitovsky,[10] and the rest were not primarily trying to develop a form of talk capable of expressing the distinctive values of the modern American activist state. Instead, the founders of contemporary welfare economics were seeking to find a place for value discourse within a profession caught up in an extreme form of positivism that called into question the meaningfulness of *any* normative judgments. In such a hostile environment, those seeking to rehabilitate the meaningfulness of normative discourse should be expected to proceed with extreme caution. Only a foolish advocate would try to persuade such an audience of the error of its ways by producing grand and inclusive theories relating principles of market exchange to a comprehensive conception of social justice. Given its positivist prejudices, the audience would simply be unwilling to suspend its disbelief for the time necessary to consider an argument as long and complex as, say, the one to be found in *A Theory of Justice.*[11]

If the advocate was to make any headway at all against the attitude that all normative judgments are arbitrary, he would have to adopt a very different rhetorical strategy, one familiar to any lawyer who has tried to convince a jury deeply suspicious of his client's cause. Rather than produce an elaborate alibi whose very complexity reinforces the jury's suspicions, the rhetorical objective is to advance a "simple" story that seems so obvious that the jury would be seduced into suspending, for a moment, its pervasive

10. Kaldor, *Welfare Propositions of Economics and Interpersonal Comparisons of Utility,* 49 ECON. J. 549 (1939); Hicks, *The Foundations of Welfare Economics,* 49 ECON. J. 696 (1939); Scitovsky, *A Note on Welfare Propositions in Economics,* 9 REV. ECON. STUD. 77 (1941).

11. J. RAWLS, A THEORY OF JUSTICE (1971).

suspicions. Given the welfare economist's particular audience, moreover, the selection of an obvious story is not very difficult. If a jury of professional economists might be induced to believe *anything,* it would accept the notion of Pareto superiority: if a trade between *A* and *B* makes nobody worse off, and at least one better off, then it is a good thing. After all, what would you think if you were going to spend your entire life describing trading behavior?

However humbling this may seem to the economist, it is only by likening him to a trial lawyer that I can account for a remarkable rhetorical anomaly in the welfare economics literature. Although the writing in this field is notorious for its formalism, subtlety, and complexity, Pareto superiority is typically presented as if it were some form of self-evident truth whose mere utterance suffices to demonstrate its validity in the manner of Revelation. Repeat after me: What could one *possibly* say against a legal change that one person thinks makes him better off when the change does not make anybody else say that he is worse off?

The answer is that there is a *lot* that could be said—a great deal, for example, about the way capitalist ideological hegemony prevents most of us from understanding our true interests. From the tone of his voice, however, the welfare economist makes it indisputably plain that he means to be asking a rhetorical question, one not to be taken seriously.[12] If he were apprised that the question was actually being taken (half) seriously by (one-eighth of) the faculty of the Harvard Law School, his most likely reaction would be shocked disbelief. Indeed, silence is probably his best response: if he actually tried to explain

12. In contrast to the normal usage in this study, "rhetoric" is advanced here as a term of opprobrium.

why he thought objections to Pareto superiority miscon-
ceived, ninety-nine times out of a hundred he would rapidly demonstrate that he was philosophically unequipped
for the task.

Do not mistake me. I do believe that Pareto superiority
is, in general, an appropriate tool for lawyerly appraisal
within a liberal legal system like ours—though even here
there are problem cases that will profit from special consideration.[13] My point is not that Pareto superiority is indefensible in serious legal conversation (indeed, I have
written a book defending it),[14] but that it is only within a
peculiar professional culture that an advocate might suc-
cessfully persuade a generally skeptical jury that the principle *needs* no defense.

Once we recognize this, we may gain some lawyerly insight into the next stage in the rhetorical development of
welfare economics. As with any other effort to articulate a
simple proposition that will serve as moral bedrock, the
problem with Pareto superiority is that it has a very limited
domain of practical application. Most real world legal arrangements generate results that, even when viewed *ex
ante,* make some people better off only at the cost of making
others worse off. As this becomes plain, only two responses
are possible.

The first is purism: as soon as the welfare economist
glimpses normative complexity, he refuses to dirty his
hands with the messy business of normative judgment.
Beyond (unquestionable) Pareto superiority, there is
nothing but a forest of subjective value judgments that

13. See, e.g., the dilemma of the Paretian liberal described by Sen in
*Liberty and Social Choice,* 90 J. PHIL. 29 (1983), and the case of Shifty
discussed at pp. 197–198 of my SOCIAL JUSTICE IN THE LIBERAL STATE
(1980).

14. See *id.,* esp. chap. 6.

have nothing to do with economics. While this is a common attitude amongst mathematical economists of the theoretical persuasion, there are bound to be more down-to-earth folks who insist on talking about the hard cases that arise in real life. Yet, since systematic normative reflection is no longer a professional option, only one response remains plausible: the path that lawyers call "reasoning by analogy."

When confronted with one of the numberless hard cases in which *V*'s legal victory means *L*'s loss, and vice versa, the applied economist need not despair. Instead, guided by his structural statement of the facts, he can glimpse a fruitful analogy between his problem case and the easy cases of genuine Pareto superiority. After all, his "statement of the facts" presents each problem case as if it were a botched bargain whose consummation has been prevented only by a set of market failures. How natural, then, to analogize the *botched* bargains that make so much normative trouble in the real world to the *perfected* bargains they might have been in the frictionless world of perfect markets? Once this analogical connection is made, the promise of relief for normative puzzlement is not far away. Just as the economist readily intuits the goodness of *real* Pareto bargains, can he not also applaud the hypothetical results of *potential* bargains? Is there really so much difference between the two cases, after all? While *L* may in fact be devastated by the losses he is asked to bear as a result of a potential Pareto improvement, the fact is that *V* would have been willing to buy *L* off were it not for the transactional obstacles blocking *V*'s way. Shouldn't the potential for a genuine Pareto improvement be enough to warrant praise of the legal change as "economically efficient"?

Moreover, so long as the applied economist is under the

thrall of his powerful analogy, he may confront hard cases with a serene self-confidence. Suppose, for example, that our applied economist is no longer analyzing a classic Coasean dispute between a single rancher and a particular farmer, but a more massive externality problem in which hundreds of Midwestern power plants discharge millions of tons of sulfur dioxide that travel a thousand miles to New England and eastern Canada before they come to earth in the form of acid rain.[15] So far as he is concerned, the massive scale, and ecological character, of the acid rain problem in no way changes the basic question of principle it raises. While estimating the amount of money the Easterners would demand in compensation may well prove a tricky business, the basic normative question is straightforward. If, in the absence of transaction costs, Midwesterners would be willing to pay off the Easterners for their acid rain damages, economic efficiency requires the law to allow them to continue their discharges downwind.

It is true, of course, that the devastated Easterners may not find much consolation in the thought of the hypothetical riches that might have been theirs in the economist's frictionless Utopia. So far as they are concerned, it is impossibly expensive to identify the particular Midwestern power plants causing particular acid rain damage, much less to bargain with them in the Coasean manner. None of this, however, disturbs the applied economist's equanimity: so long as the Midwesterners *would* be willing to pay off the Easterners in Coaseland, it is economically

15. William Hassler and I have explored the way in which Congress, the courts, and the Environmental Protection Agency have in fact responded to this characteristic problem in activist lawmaking in CLEAN COAL/DIRTY AIR (1981).

efficient to permit them to continue dumping acid rain on the East *without* compensating them in the real world. Not that the applied economist takes any great satisfaction in this dismal conclusion. Acid rain *is* a particularly humbling way to remind ourselves that there is no such thing as a free lunch, and that we cannot gain the benefits of industrial civilization without bearing its costs as well. Surely, the economist insists, it is more mature for legal decisionmakers to face up to these harsh facts of life, rather than to ignore them?

Yet, while we must forever remain mindful of the economist's truth about free lunch, the lawyer has a truth of no less importance: there is no such thing as a perfectly persuasive analogy. Indeed, the lawyer knows from long experience that a speaker can use an analogy in a rhetorically persuasive fashion only if he succeeds in inducing his audience to forget the disanalogous features of the troublesome case. After all, in contrast to the situation obtaining in the frictionless Utopia, the Easterners have not in fact bargained for anything; moreover, they emerge from their hypothetical bargain worse off than they did before they were forced into this odd kind of contract. Rather than allowing the applied economist a cheap analogy with honest-to-goodness bargaining, the lawyer insists upon a sober recognition of the differences, as well as the similarities, between the hard cases of potential Pareto optimality and the easy cases of genuine Pareto improvement: When is it fair to hold a loser to hypothetical contracts? What is so significant about contract analogies anyway? Does the applied economist wish to ground his analogy upon a deeper theory of contractarian legitimacy? If so, why? If not, what *are* the principles of political legitimacy that provide the justification for, and constraints upon, the use of hypothetical contracts as a legitimating metaphor in dispute resolution?

It is at this point, alas, that the conversation outstrips the applied economist's positivistic professional repertoire. If forced to justify his analogy, the applied economist finds himself in an awkwardly exposed position. On the one hand, he knows the purists of the profession find his efforts to extend intuitions of Pareto superiority to hard cases theoretically indefensible. On the other hand, he knows that an effort to justify his recurring invocation of hypothetical contracts will force him into some other field called political philosophy, for which he is entirely unprepared by his positivistic inheritance. How, then, to answer the challenge to the easy analogy that lies at the foundation of his appeal to economic efficiency?

My own conversations with applied economists suggest that by far the most common response at this point is some plea of confession and avoidance. What choice do I have? the applied economist asks rather plaintively. Must I really relapse into purism or lunge blindly into the undisciplined expression of subjective value judgments? It is only by speaking in terms of potentially Pareto economic efficiency that I can preserve any professional discipline at all in my talk about real world problems. Is it not appropriate for me to distinguish between those distributional judgments that are entirely beyond my professional ken and those judgments of economic efficiency upon which I can pronounce with something-like-professional-competence? True, I cannot explain to you why my guesses about the terms of hypothetical contracts made by Easterners in an unreal frictionless world ought to determine the East's real world fate. But somehow this information seems of obvious normative importance. Don't you agree?

## *Toward Law and Economics*

To be sure, activist lawyers reply, but we cannot appraise the legal value of economic efficiency until we press the conversation far beyond the point at which the applied economist is prepared to carry it. Quite simply, American lawyers emerge from a cultural tradition very different from the scientistic positivism that shaped the present orthodoxy in welfare economics. Far from declaring questions of value meaningless, lawyers aim to present the most persuasive normative account that the facts of their case and the legal materials will allow. Their task is not to suppose all values subjective, but to present arguments in a public forum in the hope that they will emerge triumphant after rigorous dialectical give-and-take. Instead of desperately searching for a couple of unproblematic intuitions that will solve all problems of value, their tradition teaches them that simple solutions are invariably simpleminded; that their first and most important duty is to confront the complexity of their legal dilemmas in a self-conscious and disciplined way; that the process of debating and refining the issues is no less important than the substantive values shaped and reshaped in the ongoing process of public dialogue. Within this cultural context, using economic efficiency as a talisman for mature legal evaluation will inevitably seem woefully naïve, no matter how sensible it seemed to the hard-headed economists struggling to find a place for value in their positivist subculture.

Not that there won't be some primitive aping of the language of applied economics by lawyers most caught up in the Coasean revolution. Just as some true believers simplify their Coasean statement of the facts by refusing to take pervasive market failure seriously, so too they may simplify their statements of value by trivializing anything that cannot be reduced to economic efficiency. It is this reductionism, of course, that accounts for so much of the Chicago school's legal notoriety.[16]

Before such a rhetorical strategy can possibly succeed, however, American law must be transformed by a political revolution equal in force to, but opposite in direction from, the one whose consequences upon the legal mind this study is investigating. Begin with the epic struggle between New Deal and Old Court that signals the constitutional triumph of the activist state. Since the fall of *Lochner* v. *New York*, American lawyers have been taught to distrust the very analogy upon which the applied economist builds his normative certainties. Where the applied economist begins with the dogmatic assertion of the unproblematic character of Pareto-superior contracts, the fate of *Lochner* cautions lawyers against placing any great

16.  It is a sign of the power of the legal culture, however, that trivialization does not come as easily to Chicago lawyers as it does to Chicago economists. Thus, while thousands of applied economists are content to use cost-benefit analysis in their practical activity, it was only an efficiency-minded lawyer like Richard Posner who thought himself obliged to *defend* economic efficiency in philosophical terms. See R. Posner, The Economics of Justice 48–115 (1981). Not that Posner's effort was particularly successful. See, e.g., the devastating critiques by Coleman, *The Normative Basis of Economic Analysis: A Critical Review of Richard Posner's The Economics of Justice*, 34 Stan. L. Rev. 1105 (1982); Dworkin, *Is Wealth a Value?* 9 J. Leg. Stud. 191 (1980); Kronman, *Wealth Maximization as a Normative Principle*, 9 J. Leg. Stud. 227 (1980). My point is, rather, that Posner remained enough of a lawyer to see that an elaborate normative defense was a conversational necessity before he could reasonably hope to convince his legal audience of the validity of his approach. In contrast, equally thoughtful Chicagoans who were interested in speaking principally to economists, rather than lawyers, persist in speaking about values in the crudest possible positivistic terms. See, e.g., Becker & Stigler, *De Gustibus Non Est Disputandum*, 67 Amer. Econ. Rev. 76 (1977).

weight on the abstract value of freedom of contract. Where the applied economist seeks to identify the contractor who would pay the most for the disputed legal right in a world of perfect markets, *Lochner* teaches us the legal folly of equating market efficiency with social justice.

To make matters worse for the Chicagoan, there is *Brown* v. *Board of Education*. While all lawyers must make their peace with *Lochner*, the terms of this accommodation may be framed negatively: thou shalt *not* imagine that perfected market justice is all there is to American law. In contrast, *Brown* forces lawyers to come to terms with an affirmative value before they can claim an understanding of the deepest aspirations of our existing legal system. Yet, when they turn to the welfare economics literature, they will search in vain for an effort to reconcile economic efficiency with *any* conception of equality. Nor will they be much comforted when they turn from the writings of professional economists to those economically minded lawyers who hope for an unproblematic translation of efficiency talk into the law. When Richard Posner, for example, was pressed to explain the evil of slavery, the best he could do was to assure us that, so long as the dollar value of our labor as free persons is higher than our dollar value as slaves, we have nothing to fear from the great god Efficiency![17]

Yet, Judge Posner has done us all a service in explicitly advancing such a trivializing account of the evil of slavery. For his example should shock us into recognizing that, so long as *Brown* v. *Board of Education* remains on the books, lawyers cannot accept his notion that judgments

17. Posner, *The Value of Wealth: A Comment on Dworkin and Kronman*, 9 J. LEG. STUD. 243, 246–247 (1980); THE ECONOMICS OF JUSTICE, *supra* note 16, at 111.

about efficiency are somehow less controversial than judgments about distribution. Within our legal culture, it seems far *less* controversial to say that slavery is wrong because it denies each person's fundamental right to equal respect, than to say that it is wrong only so long as it is inefficient. Rather than serving as an alternative to "distributional" judgments, "efficiency" is just one way of talking about the distribution of costs and benefits imposed by the legal system, and an *obviously* inadequate way of making sense of our existing legal system.[18] While the applied economist's analogy to perfected bargains might suffice to satisfy the cognitive needs of a profession operating against a bleak positivist background, it cannot serve as a conversation stopper for lawyers operating against a deeply entrenched tradition of public dialogue about individual rights and social justice. The poverty of welfare economics is especially apparent when it was *Lochner*'s insistence on the bargain principle that, only a half-century ago, threatened to destroy the standing tradi-

18. These arguments, it should be emphasized, are entirely independent of the Chicago school's effort to establish the economic efficiency of the common law. See R. POSNER, ECONOMIC ANALYSIS OF LAW 416–417, 439–441 (2d. ed. 1977). I myself find this effort entirely unpersuasive for reasons developed by Rizzo, *The Mirage of Efficiency*, 8 HOFSTRA L. REV. 641 (1980), and Priest, *Selective Characteristics*, *supra* chap. 3, note 4, among others. For present purposes, however, the substantive merit of the efficiency hypothesis as a descriptive account of the common law is secondary to the odd methodology employed by the Chicagoans. If one were interested in understanding the values expressed in *existing* American law, the place to begin is not with the common law but with the Constitution and governing activist legislation—for if these sources express ideals inconsistent with common law, every competent lawyer knows that constitutional and statutory values supersede law made by judges in a democratic system like our own. Yet not even the hardiest Chicagoan would suggest that our statutory and constitutional law display a single-minded devotion to efficiency. It is this point that serves as the crux of the critique advanced in the text.

tion of legal discourse; when it was *Brown*'s insistence upon the ideal of equality that, only a quarter-century ago, marked the greatest triumph of legality in recent American history.

## Liberal Foundations for an Activist State

In rejecting Posnerism, however, I hardly wish to encourage a professional relapse into familiar Realist musings upon the inevitable distortion and inhumanity of abstract legal thinking.[19] To the contrary: the Chicago school is absolutely right to insist that the Coasean transformation of the facts has made problematic undue reliance upon the situation sense in which the Realists took so much pride. When we try to do justice in a Constructive way that focuses upon systemic failure, no less than individual deviance, it is not enough to react intuitively to particular features of individual cases. We must also distinguish the idiosyncratic from the systemic aspects of the facts before us, and frame our legal response in the light of the structural, as well as the individual, injustices that the case may examplify.[20] Where the Chicagoans have gone wrong is

19.  For recent efforts to revive these Realist themes, see Unger, *The Critical Legal Studies Movement*, 96 HARV. L. REV. 563 (1983), as well as the work discussed in chap. 3, note 13.

20.  To forestall predictable misunderstanding, I do not believe that idiosyncrasy never counts, or that the assessment of individual responsibility for deviant actions has no place in a mature system of activist law. As Chapter 3 emphasized, one of the activist's principal preoccupations will be the effort to reconcile concerns for social justice with an abiding commitment to principles of individual responsiblity. Indeed, it has been a principal aim of my own work to present such a framework. See SOCIAL JUSTICE IN THE LIBERAL STATE, esp. sec. 42 and chap. 10 (1980). Although more work will be required to clarify the issues raised by my own

the way they propose to fill the legal vacuum left by the disintegration of Realistic situation sense. In relying so heavily on the discourse of applied economics to define the aims of activist law, they have produced a positivist parody of Constructive legal thought.

Yet even parodies have their value, if only to emphasize what Constructive lawyers cannot afford to ignore if they hope to remain faithful to their own historical traditions. Unlike the applied economist, we cannot reduce legal conversation to a guessing game about the *ex ante* bargains the parties might have reached in a frictionless Coasean world. Instead, freedom of contract makes legal sense for us within an institutional framework that guarantees individual contractors a fair share of economic power no less than political and civil rights. Only a theory that locates market freedom within this larger legitimating framework could possibly provide a general interpretive schema for an understanding of existing American law.

· 1 ·

It is this recognition, I think, that accounts for the resonant chord struck by John Rawls's *Theory of Justice* in American law schools. Rather than using hypothetical contract as a way of begging the question of the legitimate sphere of market freedom, Rawls uses the idea of contract to put the market in its place. The trick, as we all know, is to place hypothetical contractors behind a thick "veil of ignorance" and explore the ways in which they will seek to cope with the uncertainties generated by unfettered market exchange. Such a thought experiment, Rawls says, will

effort, see a forthcoming article by my colleague George Fletcher, in COL. L. REV. (1983), this is not the place to continue the work of liberal synthesis in a serious way.

reveal that competitive markets are acceptable only when controlled by an activist legal system assuring the ongoing redistribution of economic power to the worst-off classes, as well as the guarantee of civil and political freedoms of a more classically liberal character. Given this conclusion, it should be no surprise that Rawls was just the thing Constructive lawyers needed as an antidote to the abuse of applied economics. He not only provided a framework for understanding the distinctive legal structures of the American activist state. He did so in a way that encouraged lawyers to reflect upon, rather than suppress, the relationship between activist legal structures and principles of legitimacy deeply entrenched in the tradition of Western liberalism.

The Rawlsian contribution to Constructivist argument was equally important on a more technical level. Rather than celebrating the effort to ground value judgments on highly fact-dependent intuitions, Rawls takes a very un-Realistic path to the meaning of social justice in an activist state.[21] On his view, insight into our more particular intuitions will come only if we look upon them from an "original position" in which we are deprived of *all* concrete facts about our particular society. No reader of *A Theory of Justice*, moreover, could fail to be impressed by the way in which the use of a veil of ignorance can indeed transform one's prior intuitions about the nature of social justice.[22] Rather than prompting Realistic condemnation of the

21. I know of no textual indication that Rawls himself has ever seriously considered American Legal Realism in the development of his own positions.

22. For a thoughtful statement of the Rawlsian position, see Daniels, *Wide Reflective Equilibrium and Theory Acceptance in Ethics*, 76 J. PHIL. 256 (1979). For even stronger critiques of intuitionism as an appropriate form of evaluation, see B. ACKERMAN, SOCIAL JUSTICE IN THE LIBERAL STATE chap. 11 (1980); R. M. HARE, MORAL THINKING: ITS LEVELS, METHOD AND POINT (1981).

Rawlsian exercise as arid and empty, the Rawlsian thought experiment provoked deeper questions about the Constructive enterprise. Precisely because the veil of ignorance did provide a disciplined way to examine initial intuitions, it seemed important to examine Rawls's black box with a good deal of care: Did the Rawlsian construction serve as an appropriate test of one's initial intuitions? If so, why? If not, could one design a different thought experiment that *would* serve as a legitimate test?

Rawls's answer to these Constructive questions resonated deeply within our own legal tradition. His effort to reinvigorate the metaphor of a social contract had obvious connections to the historical foundations of American constitutionalism: Was not the Republic born amidst talk of social contract and individual rights? Was it not peculiarly satisfying, moreover, to put freedom of contract in its place by a complex meditation on the metaphor of contract itself?

Despite its many attractions, however, I think it would be a mistake for the profession to succumb to the image of a social contract in its ongoing effort to articulate the legal foundations of our activist state. Not that the rising forms of Constructive argument ought to deny the normative significance of contract, both actual and hypothetical, in the just resolution of a host of disputes. Nonetheless, I want to deny that bargaining metaphors ultimately do justice to our collective pursuit of activist legitimacy. Instead of defining activist justice by escaping to a never-never land that lies behind a veil of ignorance, Americans have another, better way of defining the basic terms of activist legitimacy.

It is nothing other than the process of legal disputation itself. When Americans think they have been deprived of

their rights, they characteristically express their grievances in legal terms—and insist that courts, no less than
legislatures, take their demands for justice seriously. The
beneficiaries of the status quo, moreover, are not free to
ignore their fellow citizens' legal grievances. They must
frame—on pain of a default judgment—a legally acceptable response to the question of legitimacy: What gives
you, rather than me, the right to the resource we both seek
to employ?

Just as defendants cannot respond by ignoring the
plaintiff's question, so too they are not free to rationalize
their position by offering any and every reason that might
conceivably legitimate their legal position. Instead, each
legal culture should be conceived as a vast conversational
filter that allows only a small fraction of possible justifications into the legal conversation provoked by the question
of legitimacy. It is this legally constrained conversation
that provides the cultural context to which Americans,
throughout their history, have repaired in their effort to articulate the basic nature of their collective rights against,
and duties to, one another. And it is by reflecting upon the
appropriate structure of the ongoing legal conversation,
rather than by speculating upon the terms of hypothetical
social contracts, that Constructive lawyers may be of the
greatest service to their fellow citizens.

Two features of the ongoing process of legal dialogue
should be of especial importance in the emerging Constructive understanding. The first is the *comprehensive*
legal questioning characteristic of an activist polity: rather
than presuming the sanctity of the distribution of power
generated by the basic institutions—contract, property,
family, market—thrown up by the invisible hand, the activist lawyer recognizes that any citizen disadvantaged by

the status quo may appropriately question the legitimacy of existing arrangements. To put the point in more familiar doctrinal language, my first principle of activist justice—comprehensive legal dialogue—can be viewed as a generalization of the idea of procedural due process. Whenever any person finds any of his substantial interests blocked by the legal protection of the interests of competing citizens, he has a prima facie right to demand a hearing at which he is provided with some reason explaining why the law is protecting others at his expense.[23]

And yet, while activist lawyers insist upon comprehensiveness, they also recognize the dangers involved in opening up all power structures to legal questioning. Once established power structures are stripped of their presumptively legitimate status, how is the law to check a political elite from using a momentary electoral victory as a mandate for the totalitarian overhaul of our basic institutions?[24] The question's importance, moreover, is only em-

23.   While this principle has been compromised around the edges during the past decade of Supreme Court adjudication under Chief Justice Warren Burger, even conservative commentators have doubted whether these ad hoc efforts will stand up against the force of precedent built up over the course of the past century. See Monaghan, *Of "Liberty" and "Property,"* 62 CORNELL L. REV. 405, 432–434 (1977). In any event, my argument does not depend on the precise contours of the constitutional guarantee of due process. Quite apart from the Constitution, the tendency toward comprehensive legal dialogue is expressed in countless statutes, not to speak of daily bureaucratic and judicial practice. While exceptions to the general rule do of course exist, and may even be constitutionally tolerated, this should not be allowed to conceal the central role played by comprehensive legal dialogue in the contemporary American understanding of the legitimation process. See also Mashaw, *Administrative Due Process: The Quest for a Dignitary Theory,* 61 B. U. L. REV. 885 (1981); Michelman, *Formal and Associational Aims in Procedural Due Process,* in NOMOS XVIII, DUE PROCESS (J. R. Pennock & J. W. Chapman, eds. 1977).

24.   See THE FEDERALIST NO. 10 (J. Madison).

phasized by the weakening of the old ways in which lawyers imposed conversational discipline upon the exercise of power. For, as we have seen,[25] many of the traditional features of lawyerly discourse—its focus on institutionalized expectations, individual deviance, party control, lay adjudication, finality of judgment—were organized around the continuing vitality of the *reactive constraint* and can no longer be confidently relied upon to restrain the uses of activist power.

Far from yearning for the return of a (nonexistent) golden age of reactive constraint, my own vision of Constructive lawyering is one in which the comprehensive questioning of ongoing power relationships is carried out under two constraints that prohibit totalitarian transformations. These two principles of Neutrality, developed in my book on *Social Justice in the Liberal State*,[26] are rooted in two core elements of our liberal constitutional tradition. The first principle, a generalization of the Establishment and Free Exercise clauses of the Constitution,[27] forbids citizens from justifying their legal rights by asserting the possession of an insight into the moral universe intrinsically superior to that of their fellows. The second principle, an interpretation of the Equal Protection clause,[28] forbids the legal recognition of any right that requires its holders to justify its possession by declaring themselves intrinsically superior to their fellow citizens. If I am to be

25. See Chapter 3.

26. *Supra*, note 13.

27. P. KURLAND, RELIGION AND THE LAW: OF CHURCH AND STATE AND THE SUPREME COURT (1962).

28. See, e.g., Sunstein, *Public Values, Private Interests, and the Equal Protection Clause*, 1982 SUP. CT. REV. 167 (1983); Perry, *Modern Equal Protection: A Conceptualization and Appraisal*, 79 COL. L. REV. 1023 (1979).

believed, moreover, the outcome of this constrained legal conversation will be neither a blanket endorsement of market efficiency, regardless of the inegalitarian distribution of power upon which the market is based, nor a simplistic repudiation of the ideal of free exchange, merely because it inevitably upsets any static egalitarian pattern. Instead, the upshot of liberal legal dialogue is the conditional affirmation of market freedom—conditional on the effective recognition of each citizen's right to enter the marketplace with a liberal education and a fair share of economic power. It is only within this basic structure of undominated equality[29] that the concerns of an efficiency-minded lawyer with the reduction of transaction costs and the perfection of botched bargains can take on legal value. In a world like our own, scarred by deeply entrenched patterns of poverty, racism, and sexism, this means that *lawyer*-economists cannot blandly imagine that the activist state is merely concerned with the perfection of the market structures thrown up by the invisible hand. Instead, they also must do justice to the collective aspiration to establish the social preconditions for the liberal legitimacy of the market system.

In short, instead of disciplining the activist state through an appeal to hypothetical contract, I aim to mediate ongoing political conflict through a legal culture in which public values are developed in the manner of American law, with adversaries arguing out the merits of their claims under certain fundamental conversational constraints deeply entrenched within our legal tradition. Any effort to use efficiency talk to blot out this dimension of our legal culture must be seen for what it is, a revolu-

29. The concept of undominated equality is elaborated at length in pts. 1 and 2 of Social Justice in the Liberal State, *supra* note 13.

tionary effort to blind Americans to a vital element of their standing tradition.

· 2 ·

This is not the place, though, to try to persuade you of the merits of liberal dialogue as a method of disciplining the burgeoning powers of the activist state. Indeed, it will take a generation of argument before we can begin to clarify the stakes involved in adopting one, rather than another, competing legal Construction of the pursuit of justice in an activist liberal polity. Rather than immediate clarity, the short-term prospect is the proliferation of competing Constructions.[30] For surely the notions of social contract

30. See, e.g., Ronald Dworkin's essays *What Is Equality?* (pts. 1 and 2), 10 PHIL. & PUB. AFF. 185, 283 (1981). Like Rawls and myself, Dworkin is concerned, first, to reject utilitarian solutions to the problem of distributive justice and, second, to reconcile market exchange with an underlying commitment to equality in the initial distribution of material wealth. In his work thus far, however, Dworkin has contented himself with an elaborate description of the particular egalitarian-cum-market scheme he favors. What is required, in addition, is an effort to *justify* Dworkin's particular conception of distributive justice in a way that illuminates its relationship to other fundamental aspects of the liberal tradition.

Nor will it do for Dworkin to proclaim that his favorite egalitarian formulae are rooted in our reigning political ideal of Equality of Respect, and leave the matter at that. The fact is that there are millions and millions of Americans out there who will at first deny that Equality of Respect implies initial equality in material endowments, and will insist that a proper conception of liberty or community or family is inconsistent with Dworkin's egalitarian *ipse dixits*. The challenge is to explain to such people why the principles of activist political legitimacy they *do* accept should lead them, upon reflection, to adopt egalitarian principles in areas, such as material distribution, that they initially believed should be governed by different principles. It is precisely *this* task that Rawls and I have set ourselves—by showing how larger conceptions of political legitimacy, based on social contract and liberal dialogue respectively, serve to define the rightful place of material equality and market freedom

and liberal dialogue do not exhaust the fund of legitimating ideas available to Americans seeking to make sense of their legal situation. At the very least, we may expect creative efforts to rehabilitate the utilitarian tradition that has been so unfairly eclipsed by the recent orgy of efficiency talk. There is no reason, though, for us to content ourselves with the resurrection of older philosophies. Few nations in history have ever embarked upon such a large and complex effort to reconcile the competing claims of social justice and individual freedom. Fewer still have survived a half-century without suppressing one value in the name of the other. The practical experience we gain from our successes and failures pushes us onward to a deeper understanding of the legitimating principles of liberal activism.

As our Constructive legal experience deepens and expands over time, moreover, there is every reason to expect that critical legal commentary upon it will proceed apace. Present signs indicate that these exercises in "deviationist legal doctrine"[31] will take at least two forms—one com-

---

in a just society. Until Dworkin tries to locate his own egalitarian-cum-market scheme within a larger theory of political legitimacy, it is hard for me to tell how deep our differences go on particular doctrinal issues.

It is clear enough, however, that we are of the same mind on one of the main points he addresses: rather than measuring equality in terms of each citizen's subjective sense of his own personal welfare, liberal principles should lead to a focus upon each citizen's initial share of material resources. While, in my view, this conclusion falls out of more fundamental arguments—see SOCIAL JUSTICE, *supra* note 13, secs. 13–15, and Ackerman, *What Is Neutral About Neutrality?* 93 ETHICS 372, 377–383 (1983)—it is useful to learn that this emphasis on material wealth, rather than psychic welfare, can be supported by Dworkin's more intuitionistic approach.

31. I borrow the term from Unger, *The Critical Legal Studies Movement*, 96 HARV. L. REV. 563, 576 (1983).

munitarian,[32] the other libertarian.[33] These rival efforts to prepare the way for radically different legal futures will converge upon a single critical truth: that the activist liberal present is incoherent and that the effort to build a Constructive legal understanding on such a makeshift foundation is bound to fail any thoughtful lawyer's inspection. This ongoing critique can, I think, only fuel the main line of legal activity. The best way to motivate Constructive legal work is to paint pictures of the brave new worlds that may follow upon the failure of our present enterprise in liberal activism.

I have no doubt, moreover, that liberal activists have much to learn from a serious dialogue with their critics. After all, if we are to redeem the promise of the New Deal, American lawyers can blind themselves to *neither* the lib-

---

32. The most significant theoretical text here is R. UNGER, KNOWL-EDGE AND POLITICS (1975), which bears a problematic relationship to the more applied writings associated with the critical legal studies movement, including Unger's own contribution, *supra* note 31. Compare, for example, Unger's effort in KNOWLEDGE AND POLITICS to establish the incoherence of liberalism, *id.* at 1–144, with his advocacy of "super-liberalism" in his more recent movement writings, *supra* note 31, at 602. If Unger now wishes "to remake social life in the image of liberal politics," *id.*, surely he owes us a theoretical explanation of the extent to which, and the reasons why, he has abandoned his prior judgment finding liberalism philosophically bankrupt.

33. Robert Nozick's ANARCHY, STATE AND UTOPIA (1974) is the laissez-faire manifesto that is most visible to contemporary American lawyers. I myself, however, have gotten more out of Friedrich Hayek's recent trilogy, LAW, LEGISLATION AND LIBERTY (vol. 1, 1973; vol. 2, 1976; vol. 3, 1979), and Michael Oakeshott's essays in ON HUMAN CONDUCT (1975). For serious legal critiques of activist liberalism, see R. Epstein, *supra* chap. 4, note 6; C. Fried, *supra* chap. 3, note 8. While Fried is more prone to profess sympathy with activist concerns for distributive justice than is Epstein, I myself believe that there is less of a difference between them than meets the eye. See my discussion of Fried's treatment of distributive justice in *On Getting What We Don't Deserve*, 1 J. Soc. PHIL. & POL 60 (1983).

ertarian *nor* the communitarian visions of the dissenters. The challenge instead is to grasp *both* of our critics' half-truths at the same time and build the legal foundations of a world where the affirmation of individual freedom does not conceal the pervasive reality of social injustice, where the affirmation of communal responsibility enriches the significance of personal liberty.

## · 6 ·

# The Future of
# American Law

WHAT WILL, in the end, come of all of this Constructive and critical activity?

I do not know. Perhaps ours will be the generation that witnesses the transfiguration of the activist liberal state by libertarian revival or communitarian renewal or nuclear destruction. If so, lawyers will have to make their Realistic peace with the new New Deal as best they can, or quit the law for more pressing engagements.

But perhaps we will have the chance for more Constructive work and help redeem the promises made a half-century ago: that it is possible to understand social reality well enough to improve upon the invisible hand; that it is possible to use the awesome power of an activist state to enrich, rather than parody, the American commitment to liberty and justice for all. If this does prove to be our calling, I am prepared to make a single prediction: lawyers who persist in their Realist wisdom will fail to redeem the promise of the New Deal.

My prophecy is based upon the patent shift in the balance of professional power that is taking place all around us. At the dawn of the New Deal, lawyers had two professional assets that assured them a commanding place within the emerging activist state. The first was professional prestige—all the more valuable in a democratic society skeptical of the traditional bases of authority.[1] The second was sheer numbers. To put it bluntly, only the legal profession was producing thousands of people each year who, after seven years of university education, might be counted on to write a reasonably persuasive paragraph or even organize a persuasive argument.

As we celebrate the New Deal's half-century, however, it is quite plain that this era of professional hegemony is coming to a close. As they scramble toward the heights of public and private power, lawyers are increasingly encountering new professional competitors: economists, public policy analysts, management consultants, computer scientists. These technocratic newcomers can also bask in the dim glow of professional degrees bestowed by the finest universities in the land—M.B.A. not LL. B., Ph.D. not J.D. They too advance by the thousands to claim their rightful place of leadership in the activist state. Indeed, there is only one obvious difference between them and us. While they may often be unable to write a persuasive English paragraph, they can come up with a persuasive-looking computer program, stating the facts with a seeming rigor we are ill-equipped to match.

1. See, e.g., M. S. LARSON, THE RISE OF PROFESSIONALISM: A SOCIOLOGICAL ANALYSIS (1977).

Within this context of interprofessional competition between technocrats and lawyers, Realist wisdom has a very different implication for professional survival than it did during the precomputer era in which it first triumphed. During the first half-century of the New Deal, Realism provided an essential means by which the profession could disengage from its laissez-faire past without undue damage to its rhetorical repertoire. During the next half-century, continuing distrust of formalism will imply a professional failure to acquire the skills of statistical inference and econometric analysis that will seem increasingly essential to the reasoned exercise of activist authority in the twenty-first century. This failure, in turn, implies that lawyers will emerge from the interprofessional competition for power in a vastly diminished condition.

The nature of the change can best be expressed through Bagehot's famous distinction between the dignified and the efficient aspects of constitutional government.[2] At the present moment, the legal profession still occupies a hegemonic position in both of these essential dimensions of political ascendancy. Lawyers preside over the dignified processes of legislative enactment and judicial review; they also dominate the efficient processes of discretionary administration and implementation of activist regulation. It is on this second level that the profession will suffer its most striking setbacks if it persists in its Realist thought-ways. Deprived of a capacity to state the facts in a professionally disciplined fashion, lawyers will be increasingly confronted with technocratic rivals who suffer under no such professional inhibition, who will be only too happy to describe the present and project the future in an

2. W. BAGEHOT, THE ENGLISH CONSTITUTION 4–8 (2d ed. 1872).

endless stream of computer printout. Lost in this sea of numbers, it will become harder and harder for Realistic lawyers to oppose their shaky sense of the situation to the masses of impressive-looking stuff streaming out of the computer. It will come to seem increasingly pigheaded to condemn one or another technocratic action as an abuse of discretion meriting correction through an appeal to the lawyers' symbolic powers in Congress and the courts. Indeed, over time, even these last institutional bastions of legal dignity will suffer erosion: however political the legislative process, however intuitionistic adjudication, surely a cogent statement of the facts is not altogether irrelevant? Increasingly lawyers in Congress and the courts will find themselves surrounded by technocrats whose voices they will constantly be tempted to parrot, however Realistically.

And what, it might well be asked, is wrong with that? Whoever said that lawyers ought to preside forever at the helm of the American activist state? After all, if we lift our eyes from North American shores, we shall find that activist states across the Atlantic and the Pacific seem to be doing well enough, thank you, without the legions of lawyers who have managed to encumber the new colossus. Is it not time to send the lawyers back where they belong, tending the inevitable problems of reactive justice that will endure as part of the larger activist enterprise?

Good questions, to which there can be no final answers. No tradition can be expected to survive, let alone prosper, if its adepts are unwilling to engage in the ongoing work of reconstruction. Each generation must be prepared to express the living values of American law in a way that makes sense of the changing facts of American life. Although I have no doubt that the path of reconstruction marked in this book is full of unseen dangers, as well as hidden opportunities, this is hardly the first time that

American lawyers have confronted similar perplexities. Indeed, as we reflect upon the use we will make of our historical situation, we may finally come to a renewed respect for the legal achievements of our Realist predecessors. Even as we reject their solutions, we cannot help but admire their refusal to retreat in shocked silence before the activist state, their insistence that, somehow or other, lawyers *could* make sense of the brave new world in which they and their fellow citizens found themselves. It is only because of the Realists' success in stabilizing a credible form of legal discourse during the past half-century that Constructive lawyers may even imagine the possibility of reworking the legal tradition in ways that make a deeper sense of the activist state. Will our children be able to say the same about us?

If not, they will find little reason to rejoice in the fall of the American legal mind from the heights of power. Other countries have other traditions upon which they may rely to civilize the powers of technocracy and channel them into constructive ends. If Americans lose their moorings in the law, however, it will not be so easy for them to develop the modes of discourse that take law's place in England or Germany, Japan or Russia. Instead, our fellow citizens may well celebrate the New Deal's centenary within a power structure effectively governed by technocrats operating under the thinnest veneer of Realistic legalism. And that, I am convinced, would be a very bad thing. For however skilled the computer analysts of the future become in finding relevant facts, I see very few signs of a reawakening of the technocratic mind from its positivist slumbers. Instead, my conversations with M.B.A.'s and M.P.A.'s and Ph.D.'s in universities, industry, and government have often revealed a commitment to a kind of value-discourse so primitive and vulgar that it would make even Chicago school lawyers blush. At least the Chicagoans make an effort to convince us that their talk of efficiency can make sense of our legal traditions; at least they are aware of the need to convince the rest of us of the substantive merit of efficiency in an ongoing public dialogue.[3] In contrast, many, though one hopes not most, technocrats have been stripped by their positivist education of even this much respect for our standing traditions of governance. The very idea that one ought to defend efficiency in an ongoing public debate leaves them perplexed: What more can I possibly say in praise of efficiency after I have said I like it even better than apple pie?

Whatever the failings of American lawyers, they know that there *is* something more that must be said by those who hope to legitimate the exercise of authority, even as they disagree on what that Something is. It is precisely this professional commitment to public dialogue that must remain at the foundation of the activist state if it is not one day to collapse upon us all in some awful form of technocratic tyranny. The mere fact that the liberal activist state has survived to 1984 is, doubtless, consoling, but it should not blind us to the dangers all Americans run if lawyers persist in a shallow Realism that has outlived its time.

Not that a vigorous and constructive legal dialogue can ever hope to compensate for an apathetic and muddled political debate. Yet the reverse is also true: political commitment is no substitute for legal deliberation. While the future of America depends on the American people, the future of American law depends, in a special way, on the way American lawyers interpret their calling.

3. See *supra* chap. 5, note 16.

# Index

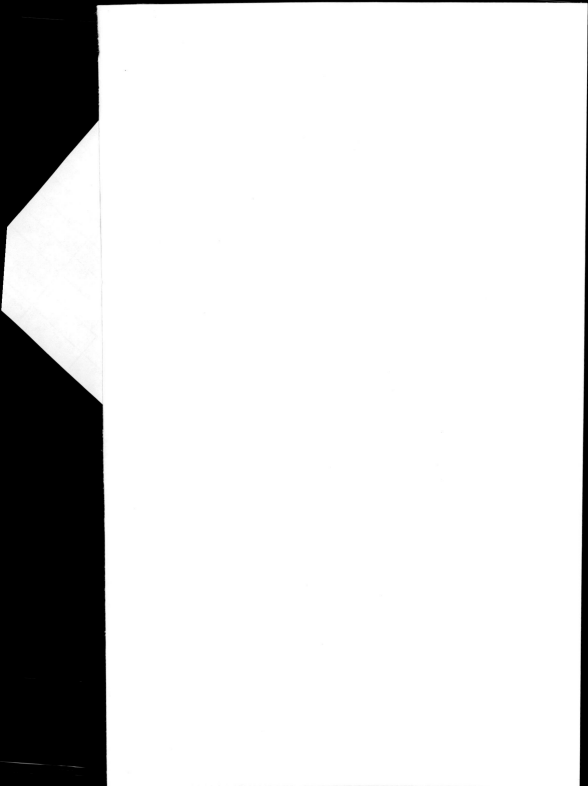

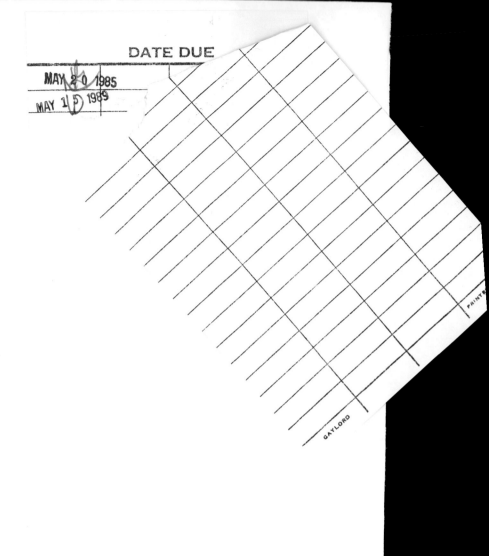

GAYLORD